If You Had Listened To Grandma, You Wouldn't Need A Shrink!

No psychobabble … just plain old fashioned wise advice

Sheila Lazarus, PhD
a.k.a.
Dr. Grandma

AuthorHouse™
1663 Liberty Drive
Bloomington, IN 47403
www.authorhouse.com
Phone: 1-800-839-8640

© 2011 Sheila Lazarus, PhD. All rights reserved.

No part of this book may be reproduced, stored in a retrieval system, or transmitted by any means without the written permission of the author.

First published by AuthorHouse 10/19/2011

ISBN: 978-1-4567-6735-8 (sc)
ISBN: 978-1-4567-6737-2 (e)
ISBN: 978-1-4567-6736-5 (hc)

Library of Congress Control Number: 2011907999

Printed in the United States of America

Any people depicted in stock imagery provided by Thinkstock are models, and such images are being used for illustrative purposes only. Certain stock imagery © Thinkstock.

This book is printed on acid-free paper.

Because of the dynamic nature of the Internet, any web addresses or links contained in this book may have changed since publication and may no longer be valid. The views expressed in this work are solely those of the author and do not necessarily reflect the views of the publisher, and the publisher hereby disclaims any responsibility for them.

Erma Bombeck

June 23, 1986

Dear Sheila:

    Please forgive me for taking so long to answer your beautiful letter (which, by the way, I had no difficulty at all reading). I am touched that you would take the time - and the precious energy - to write.

    I don't pretend to know even half of what a handicapped mother goes through. I would like nothing better than to read Sheila Lazarus's book about it one day. In the meantime, know there is a writer out there who thinks you are very courageous.

                           Love,

                           Erma Bombeck

This book is dedicated to my beloved children,
Lance and his wife, Yolanda,
and Nicole and her husband, David.
Also to my grandchildren,
Isabella, Alexandra, and Andre Lazarus,
and Jacob Shipitofsky,
without whom I could not have become Dr. Grandma.

Acknowledgments

I wish to thank my late maternal grandmother, Celia Pelovsky, who was blind but taught me to see the world so clearly through her wisdom.

In addition, I want to thank my late aunt, Jennie Neustadter, for helping me to write my first book report. She would be so proud of me.

Next, I would like to thank my mother-in-law, Mitzi Lazarus, who is as wise as my own grandmother was. She is ninety-five years old and can always be found out and about with her boyfriend, Sam, who is also in his nineties. She is a great-grandmother to Zack, Chelsea, Isabella, Alexandra, Andre, Jacob, and Minnie. They all love to spend time with her. Great-grandma posed as the model for this book. Since she loves motorcycling, it was easy to select the photo for the front cover of the book.

Also, I want to thank all of my patients at Century House, Riverview Medical Center in Red Bank, New Jersey, for encouraging me to put my grandmother's words on paper and into a book for all the world to see.

Last but not least, I would like to thank the love of my life, my husband Larry. While our life's journey has been challenging, he has always been loyal and deeply devoted to me and our family. Above all, he has been by my side for forty-four years and has loved me even in the early years of our marriage, when he did not understand who I really was. As my best friend, he is the person with whom I want to grow old while staying young at heart.

My Bubbie

Table of Contents

Respect	2
Letting Go	7
Holding On	12
Inspiration	15
Love	21
Spirituality	27
Self and Others	34
Anger	39
Conflict Resolution	46
Boundaries	52
Solving Problems and Making Decisions	55
Preparation, Thinking Ahead, and Setting Goals	61
Anxiety and Coping Mechanisms	69
Assertiveness	73
Fear	76
Sadness	81
Irrational Thinking and Thought-Stopping	88
Defense Mechanisms	93

Stress and Relaxation	97
Self-Esteem	105
Change	109
Loss and Grief	113
Enjoy Life … Happy Thoughts … Status	120
Health, Personal Hygiene, and Moderation	126
Manners	130
Diversity and Discrimination	136
Being Gullible	141
Communication and Effective Listening	147
Let's Have Fun, Just You and Grandma	153
Taking Responsibility	157
Procrastination	161
Encouragement and Support	165
Being Grateful and Giving Thanks	171
Mind Your Own Business	174
How to Handle Money	177
Life's Lesson's	181

Disclaimer

Yiddish sentences and phrases may not be exact in terms of wording, punctuation, and grammar. They merely represent the gist of what my grandmother was saying.

Preface

When I was a little girl, my grandmother was the most important person in my life. She was a wonderful and courageous woman who came from Eastern Europe with her husband and her younger brother, Joe. Though she was blind, she taught me to see the world very clearly. Every time I saw her she would say something that I thought was important—I wasn't sure how important at the time. Sometimes she said the following words in Yiddish: *"Azar Zeiseh maideleh, di, mazel, mazel, dos, abi gezunt."* When I asked my parents to translate, something was lost. The literal version was, "Sweet girl, luck, luck, as long as there is health." Even though the words themselves did not make complete sense to me, I understood the gist of what she was saying. She was extolling my virtues as a young lady and hoped that my life would be filled with joy, good luck, and, above all, good health. It seems that good luck and good health were priorities for my grandmother, and for Jewish people in general. Throughout my childhood I kept a diary of her broken sentences and advice to me. I still cherish that diary, even though the pages are wrinkled and yellow with age.

When I worked as a social worker in a drug and alcohol rehabilitation center in New Jersey, I counseled many patients who were in detox and unable to easily grasp the usual psychobabble that was spewed by the counselors. In order to make the concepts simple and understandable, I began to use phrases from my diary that my grandmother had passed down to me. The patients responded in a positive manner and began to repeat my grandmother's words to each other.

My grandmother was a very positive individual who believed that there would be a tomorrow, a tomorrow in which change could take place. She did not dwell on the past and always encouraged me to *let go* of unproductive thoughts and behaviors. Sometimes I would complain, over and over, about an argument that I had with a friend at school. While she helped me to process my anger, she also encouraged me to look forward instead of backward. She often said,

"*Shelenkeh, shelenkeh, genug is genug, morgn afdernakht.*" ("Enough, enough. Tomorrow before midnight it will be a thing of the past.")

Because my patients tended to focus on their unchangeable issues of the past, I began teaching the concept of *letting go of the past* through my grandmother's words: *"Genug is genug, morgn afdernakht."* My patients loved hearing the guttural sounds of the Yiddish words. They always converted the Yiddish into English words, phrases, or names that they could easily recall. For this particular phrase, the patients substituted the words, *Gene Morgan*.

One day I overheard two patients talking to each other. One of the patients had been *stuck* in the past. Her cohort was trying to help her to look ahead instead of backward. I was shocked and pleasantly surprised when I overheard the following words: "You know what Sheila's grandmother would say to you—Gene Morgan."

I was so thrilled; my grandmother's words lived on! The patients loved how easy it was to understand an important concept that they had learned in Yiddish. They suggested that I write a book of my grandmother's sayings, because they thought it would be helpful to all people, not just to those in rehab. Ergo, this book.

Looking forward instead of backward was not the only wisdom that my grandmother passed on to me. When I was about eight years old I learned to ride a bicycle. I was so excited. I was required to abide by my mother's rule: ride only on the sidewalk. My house was at the bottom of a hill, and I enjoyed riding up and down the hill. The more secure I felt on the bicycle, the faster I pedaled. Once, when I was passing a house surrounded by a brick wall, I was unable to slow down enough. I scraped my leg along the entire brick wall and then ran home screaming and bleeding.

When my mother heard me crying she came to the door. Even though she saw that I was hysterical, she merely told me to go into the bathroom, wash my leg off, and put a Band-Aid on it. My grandmother heard me crying and came into the bathroom. Even though she could not see the bleeding, she lightly touched my knee and felt the blood.

She looked straight into my eyes and gave me a hug. She did not say anything, but it was as though she could look into my soul with her eyes. How could she do that and be blind? I didn't know. All I knew was that once my grandmother looked into my eyes with such love, I felt calm, safe, and secure.

She lovingly washed my leg and bandaged it and said, *"Biz chasseneh, abi gezunt."* ("Until the wedding, as long as there is health.") She was essentially telling me that it would heal well; by the time that I got married, the incident would be a thing of the past. Since that day, whenever I talk to people I make sure that I look deep into their eyes so that they feel important and safe.

Even today, I think of my grandmother when I am fearful and need to feel the safety and security of her warm hugs. I have undergone many surgeries in my lifetime. The night before a surgery was always traumatic, cold, frightening, and lonely. I always wanted my grandmother to be with me during those stressful times, but she had already passed away. To compensate, I decided to look over my right shoulder and see her in my mind's eye. Her gaze always made me feel so safe. And now, even today, when I want to access my grandmother, I still look over my right shoulder and feel her presence in my life. My grandmother nurtured me, and as a result she taught me how to nurture others and make them feel good about themselves.

While all of the sayings presented in this book might not be exactly literal, the concepts that my grandmother passed down to me have helped me during the good and bad times in my life, and I hope they will help you. My goal in writing this book is to help others learn to love the life they live. Having a loving advocate in one's life who provides lots of hugs, loving gazes, and pats on the back is invaluable for enhancing self-esteem. Unfortunately, we cannot buy, rent, or borrow self-esteem from others. It must come from within. And so I encourage anyone who is reading this book to say to him- or herself on a daily basis, "I am a wonderful person, and I love myself." My grandmother will be your guiding angel until you learn to truly love yourself.

Grandma's Favorites
*Lots of love, lots of hugs, lots of support ...
and lots of chicken soup!*

Respect

Respect means many different things. It involves giving serious worth and value to other people's thoughts, feelings, needs, ideas, wishes, and preferences. But respect is much more than mere consideration of others. It includes listening and acknowledging others by accepting their individuality and idiosyncrasies. Respect cannot be demanded; it must be earned. My grandmother taught me how to respect others, how to be respected, and, above all, how to respect myself.

When I was about ten years old, my family went to Pittsburgh to visit relatives. We decided to go shopping in the local town. Because there were so many of us, we went by bus, not by car. At one particular stop, a pregnant woman entered the bus. Because there were no available seats, she stood in front of my grandmother. The woman's body brushed against my grandmother, who then realized that the woman was pregnant and without a seat. She immediately said to my brother, *"Onkukn."* ("Give a look over there.") Her words indicated that my brother should offer his seat to the woman, which he did. The woman was grateful.

At another stop, an old woman with bags of groceries entered the bus. She also stood in front of my grandmother, who could feel the woman's bags of groceries at her feet. I realized that I was next on my grandmother's list. She said, *"Shelenkeh, onkukn."* ("Sheila, give a look over there.") This was my cue to give my seat to the elderly lady with the bags of groceries. Another seat later opened up, and I sat down. When I saw another old woman entering the bus I simply gave my seat up to her without any prompting from my grandmother. When the first old woman got up to leave the bus, she came over to me and gave me a hug. I felt so happy then that I'd taken the time to acknowledge another person's plight. By making the old woman happy, I made myself happy. As my brother and I stepped off the bus, my grandmother held her hand up in the air and whispered to both of us, *"Seier gut"* ("Very good.") We knew that she was proud of us; as a result, we were proud of ourselves as well. We felt respected.

My grandmother taught me to look beyond myself and to be concerned for others. She encouraged me to respect what other people say, even if I disagree with the thought. I now tend to listen carefully to what others are saying and clarify any issue that may be in question. As a result, friends, relatives, and patients tend to perceive me as very attentive. They often say things to me in the following vein: "You know, you really care about what I am saying. That's great! Nowadays people just don't care much about other people!" And I find that when people respect one another, there are fewer conflicts.

What Grandma said:

You don't buy respect ... you earn it.

Treat others the same way you want to be treated.

The world doesn't revolve just around you.

Respect your sister, brother, mother, and father.

No man is an island, and don't you forget it.

Don't be selfish; think of somebody else's feelings.

Honesty is good, but some things keep to yourself.

If you haven't something good to
say, keep your mouth shut.

Don't worry about winning or losing; you
should be nice during the game.

Don't say a bad word about our country.

Respect our president; he (maybe one
day she) takes care of our world.

Always remember the golden rule.

What Grandma said:

Be kind to animals.

Respect your elders.

Don't talk back; it's not nice.

Knock before you go in.

Don't stay too long in bathroom; others have to go, too.

Don't bite the hand that feeds you.

Don't ever read your sister's diary; it's private.

Respect your teacher.

Don't stare.

No shouting; speak nicely!

Never be mean to the dog.

Listen to what someone else has to say.

Don't hog the conversation.

Memory:

After the bus ride that I described earlier, my grandmother remained elated for the whole day. At dinner that night, she looked at me and my brother and said to us, "Derech-erez sich, anderer, wichti." ("Respecting yourself, others, is important.") She was trying to tell us that respect could not be bought or sold. Rather, it was something that you earned through your own actions. And once you had it, you had it all of your life, and it was a great thing to have!

Letting Go

We often hang onto toxic thoughts that can live rent-free within our brain. These toxic thoughts consume psychic energy that could be utilized in more positive ways. When I was a little girl I remember being very angry at my girlfriends, who were being catty, as little girls often are. My grandmother often heard me lamenting about how upset and angry I was over particular incidents that had occurred. When I was about nine years old, I attended a nearby local elementary school. In those days parents did not fear for the lives of their children when they walked to school. Since my house was on the way to the school, my three friends came to my door to pick me up every morning. One day as I was looking out of my window for my friends, I saw them walk past my house. I was astounded that they did not even look in my direction. I started to cry, and I threw my lunchbox on the floor. My grandmother just stood next to me and did not say one word. After I screamed for five minutes, unable to use my voice, she calmly said in Yiddish, *"Genug, kopweitik, morgn nischt selbik!"* ("Enough already—stop, you're giving me a headache. Tomorrow won't be the same!")

Essentially, she was telling me to stop looking back and to look forward, because tomorrow would probably be different and much better for me. It was. The next day my friends came to my door, and all was well again!

What Grandma said:

Don't make no business; forget about it.

Stop complaining! Enough is enough—
you give me headaches.

It can't rain forever.

Give it up ... move on, already.

I'm sick of hearing the same old thing.

Don't pay any attention to him/her; let it
go in one ear and out the other.

Let the dog sleep and lie there.

Don't look back; look ahead.

Don't cry if you already spilled the milk.

Stop driving yourself crazy.

What Grandma said:

I don't want to hear about that any more, do you understand?

Forget about it already!

You can lead a horse to water but you can't make him drink it.

Stop trying to get him to change; he never will.

Soon, it will be a thing of the past, and you won't even think about it.

Don't waste any more good energy on that; it won't help.

Listen, you can't find a needle in a haystack; so stop looking already.

It doesn't do you any good to keep crying over it; do something else.

Memory:

I remember coming home from school one day with a bad grade. I had always received excellent marks, but apparently I was unprepared for that surprise quiz that my teacher had given the class. I was crying hysterically and kept saying, "I hate school." My mother was unsympathetic and told me that I deserved the bad grade because I did not study, which made me feel even worse. When my grandmother came along she told me, "Genug!" ("Enough!") She meant that crying was not going to improve my grade, because it had already happened. She made me calm down, gave me a hug, and told me to watch television for a little while. Once she realized that I was more relaxed, she encouraged me to study hard in case there was another surprise quiz the next day. I took her advice and worked diligently. There was another surprise quiz, and I earned my usual A. I finally stopped the complaints and focused on my assignments every night. I learned that psychic energy is very precious and should not be wasted on something unproductive.

Holding On

While we must sometimes learn to *let go*, other times we must learn to *hold on*. While the former involves surrendering, the latter involves persevering, even in the face of great challenges and diversities. The trick is in knowing which to pick in a given situation, letting go or holding on. My grandmother helped me to understand the difference between the two.

I realized that if something had already happened and I could not change it, even though it made me angry, I was to let it go. One day I lost a beautiful bracelet that I had received for a gift. I lamented over it for days and days. My whole family looked for it but to no avail. My grandmother said to me, *"Ophaltn eider grays deign."* ("Stop before there is a big worry.") What she was trying to tell me was that I needed to let that go. There were bigger worries in the world, and I should stop making such a big deal over something that I could not change.

On the other hand, it was clear when she wanted me to persevere in the face of adversity. When I was about seven years old my father taught me how to ride a two-wheeled bicycle. My grandmother was there and overheard my dad telling me to hold on and keep pedaling. I tried many times but continued to fall off. My father went into the house and told me to keep practicing by myself. I was very frustrated. How could I do it on my own if I couldn't do it with my father's help?

My grandmother remained outside with me and said, *"A klog iz mir, farsorgn, tretl, nisht geferlech, a shtik naches."* ("Keep pedaling, there have been worse; you'll find great pleasure.") She was trying to tell me that there are many challenges in life and that in the face of adversity I must *hold on* so that I will be pleased with my perseverance and accomplishment in the end. I remained steadfast in my determination and was riding the bicycle myself one hour later. I was so happy that I had not given up! Even today, I remain steadfast in the face of great adversity. Thanks, Bubbie.

What Grandma said:

Steady effort wins the race, so stay in the race and run.

You've come so far; don't give up now.

Just keep hanging on; don't give up the ship.

Come on, you can do it.

Grandma's here, so keep going!

You better fight until the bitter end.

Keep going, swim and there will be no sink.

If there's really nothing you can do
about it, move on, move on.

Try to keep up; I know you can do it—just a little more.

If you don't get it right first, so do it again.

Memory:

I remember doing a school project in which I had to draw a vase. That was the easy part. The hard part was making paper flowers and placing them atop the vase. My flowers kept falling off the sheet time and time again. I was so frustrated that I yelled, "No more!" My grandmother was very calm and just told me, "Bubbie do, du machn." ("Grandma is here, you can do anything.") She was letting me know that I could accomplish anything I wanted to, as long as I persevered. And so I kept trying until I made some colorful flowers that enhanced my vase. I knew that she believed in me, and I never wanted to disappoint her. I never forgot that incident. Her words inspire me, even today, both in my personal and professional lives.

Inspiration

In order to survive, thrive, and achieve our goals we need a vision of hope for our future. Sometimes our minds are sparked by a sudden intuition that arouses a particular emotion or action. This spark may come from a charismatic individual, from music, from literature, or from film.

For me, the inspiration came from listening to a song and listening to my grandmother. When I was about eleven years old I used to listen to Frank Sinatra's song "Fly Me to the Moon." I loved it so much that I played it over and over; my grandmother and I sang it all the time. My grandmother once said to me, *"Eins tog du holemn alzdig meglech."* ("One day anything will be possible.") She was trying to tell me that all things are possible if you work hard, if you are creative and imaginative, and if you don't give up. Her spark inspired me to undertake many things that I found to be frightening.

When I worked in the addiction center I often told my patients that my grandmother had inspired me as we sang songs that had important words to reflect upon. And so I often played a reflective Frank Sinatra song for them called "Look Down the Lonesome Road," followed by an inspirational Barry Manilow song called "I Made It Through the Rain." My patients looked forward to the music. We often discussed how the songs affected us. Since my patients knew that the idea for the songs emanated from my grandmother, whom I called Bubbie, the patients usually left the group session saying, "Thank you, the Bubbie of Sheila!" She lived again through my patients. This caused me great joy because it reflected my original intention to impart my grandmother's wisdom to my patients.

What Grandma said:

Every cloud has silver or gold in it.

It's always darkest before the morning comes.

Look on the bright side of things.

The good thing about the bottom
is you can go to the top.

In the morning it will look better, you'll see.

A good cry will make you feel better … it's okay.

No matter how bad it is you can always
tell me … I'll be there for you.

Keep a stiff lip on the top.

Make do with happy thoughts.

I know you can do it; keep trying.

Make a steady effort to win a race.

Count your blessings.

Memory:

I remember when a friend's mother bought her a pair of boots that were the latest craze. I thought that I would die if I didn't have them for myself. I kept asking my mother to buy them for me, and she simply looked at me and shook her head no. My grandmother told me, "Reichen gut." ("Be grateful.") She was telling me that I had much more than many others and that I should be grateful for what I did have and not lament over what I did not have. She wanted me to understand that there would always be those who had more than I did, as well those who had less than I did.

This served me well as an adult. When my children were small, I became chronically ill. I was homebound for a very long time. I felt quite isolated and very much alone. I encouraged my husband to travel with the children so that they would not become impacted by my illness. When I heard the song "Fly Me to the Moon," I remembered my grandmother's wisdom. I was grateful for what I could do ... talk on the telephone. And so, inspired by both the song and my grandmother's wisdom, I created the first of its kind: a telephone support group for handicapped mothers. It was called Comfort Call of Greater New Jersey. Not only did I help myself, but I helped those other mothers who were in a similar situation. We created a chain of strength!

What Grandma said:

The bird that's early catches the worm.

On me, you can always count.

Let me kiss the *boo boo*.

Remember, you can tell Grandma anything.

It's a good idea to love a neighbor.

Give it your best try; you can do it.

Always look on the bright side of things.

Remember, tomorrow will come again.

I know you can do it if you keep trying.

Really put your mind to it; you'll get it done.

What Grandma said:

Let Grandma read you a beautiful poem.

Get a good night's sleep; everything
will look better in the morning.

Give thanks.

Have faith.

Let's hope.

You don't get more than you can chew, believe me.

Look up; make a wish on a star.

Always have a dream, because
dreams maybe will come true.

Memory:

When I was about nine years old I had a dance recital. My grandmother always sat on my bed in my room while I practiced my routine. Even though she could not see what I was doing, she sensed the movements and moved her hands back and forth in time to the music. She was very excited to come to my dance recital. I often wondered why she would be so happy to come when she could not even see the stage. She was my greatest cheerleader. She was so proud that I was going to be on stage, to be her little Sheila, the dancer. Before I went on stage she told me, "Eins tog efscher tenser, bale." ("Maybe one day a real dancer, a ballerina.")

Needless to say, I made several blunders. When my peers were going to the right, I was moving to the left. After the recital, my mother said that my dancing was good except for when I made the mistakes. There was a hush. My grandmother immediately came over to give me a hug and said to me, in her broken English, "You want, asoi pruw." ("You really want, try more.") She was trying to tell me that if I really wanted to be a dancer, if that was my dream, I should keep taking lessons to see what might come of it. While she did not tell me that I would become a prima ballerina, she did give me the inspiration and encouragement to pursue my dancing, as in ballroom dancing. My husband and I have done competitive ballroom dancing, and we have achieved many first-prize trophies. If only my Bubbie could have been there to see her little Shelenkeh, the dancer.

Love

We all need love; it makes the world go around and around. Love is a strong, positive emotion that involves deep devotion, positive feelings of affection, and intense regard. One can both love and be loved. *Beloved* is the term of endearment for one who is loved. Love often involves hugs, kisses, and nurturing from another individual … especially from Grandma. Love means warmth and fuzziness, security, and nurturing. My grandmother showed me love. She didn't just say that she loved me, but she showed me that she loved through her touch. She often took my face in her hands and traced the outlines of my eyes, nose, and mouth. She would say to me, *"Shelenhkeh, shelenkeh, siskeit, siskeit, mazel."* ("My Sheila, my Sheila, such sweetness, sweetness; have good luck.") Her touch was so magical that I felt a shudder of love radiate through my whole body.

Since she could not see to read, I would often read books to her. She always sat next to me and put her arm around my shoulder. She listened intently and often nodded her head to indicate that she understood. As I read to her, she often gave feedback, saying, *"Sheelenkeh, zaier gut."* ("My Sheila, very good.") She always made me feel important and special and good about myself.

I tried to replicate that scenario with my own children when they were young. I read a little and then they read a little. I sat very close to them and praised them. I guess the children felt loved by me as I had felt loved by my grandmother. When they were little I often traced the outlines of their faces with my fingers and used my grandmother's words. To my son I said, "Lance, Lance, *siskeit, siskeit, mazel*" ("Lance, Lance, my sweetness, have luck"), and to my daughter I said, "Nicole, *siskeit, siskeit, mazel*." ("Nicole, Nicole, my sweetness, have luck.")

I think that I taught my children how important it was to love and be loved. Throughout the years I have suffered with many chronic illnesses. Often, I was sad. On many occasions, my young daughter Nicole would come over to me, put her little arms around my neck, and say to me, "Mommy, I love you; I will read to you and make you better." My daughter's Girl Scout leader told me that at the end of every meeting there was a final closing circle, and each scout could make a wish. My daughter's wish was invariably that her mommy would have good health. Both of my children express their love for their families in a way that my grandmother would have loved so much!

What Grandma said:

Don't worry, Grandma loves you.

Come here, Grandma needs a hug.

Memory:

My grandmother was making herself a glass of hot tea. She did that daily, usually without a mishap. She even poured the hot tea into her glass by herself. But one day, she miscalculated and spilled the tea all over the table and the floor. I could see that she was upset. I told her that I would clean it up and that it was easy for me. I did not want her to feel badly. After I cleaned the mess, I told her that everything was as good as before. She stood there in silence for a moment. I had no idea what she was going to do or say. The next thing I knew, she was asking me to come over to her and give her a hug. It seemed as though I was the reason that she felt better. I was so happy to make her happy. The hug oozed with love.

One day when working in the addiction center, I encountered a patient who was eighty-five years old. In a group session, she began to cry. She told the group that nobody had ever given her a hug. I told the group that my grandmother would have lined up all of the people in the group and have them give her a hug … which is what I did. Her response was, "Sheila, this is the best day of my life!" Hugs do not cost anything, so give them freely. They offer a deep connection of affection. Just remember, love does help to make the world go 'round!

What Grandma said:

Give Grandma a nice big kiss.

You look so handsome! I love you so much.

My poor baby, Grandma loves you.

I am so proud of you; come, I'll give you a hug.

Come get a hug; I'll wipe away your tears.

Somebody up there loves you, so always look to the sky!

I love you sssooo mmmuuucccchhhh!

What's life when there is no love? Not good.

People—people, they need each other.

Memory:

During my daughter's Bat Mitzvah, I was so proud of the way that she read her Torah. Parents were allowed to say a few words to their child while on the Bema (ceremony stage). I thought and thought of what I would say to her. When I thought about what my grandmother would say to me, I immediately knew what I was going to do. I told Nicole that I felt the presence of her great-grandmother. I explained that if my grandmother had been there, she would have placed her hands on my daughter's face and traced the outline of her features.

And in the absence of my grandmother, I told my daughter that I was going to perform the same task. I slowly traced my daughter's face, feeling her eyebrows, nose, and mouth, and I said, "From my Bubbie in Yiddish, 'Libe, Mazel mein kind, mazel.' ("May love and good luck follow you forever.") There was a hush in the audience. I heard sniffles and saw one lone tear fall from my daughter's eye. I knew that my grandmother was watching over us. Lastly I said to her, "And from me in English, I love you deeper than the ocean, higher than the sky, and more than M & Ms!" My daughter then gave me the tightest hug ever ... and the whole audience cried!

Spirituality

The great mystics of the world are on a quest for spirituality, the search to discover their innermost essence. The foundation of this quest is to find our true selves and discover the real nature of consciousness. We seem to remain ignorant of this deeper identity that we all actually possess. For my grandmother, spirituality was not tangible; rather, it was something mystical and enigmatic. I knew that it was very important because she often talked to me about it before bedtime.

My grandmother would come into my bedroom, sit on my bed, and say, *"Derwackseiner haloime."* ("Adult talk.") I knew that she wanted to talk to me about what I wanted to be when I grew up. I always sensed that there was more to her conversation than she would admit. We talked about my aspirations for college and maybe becoming a teacher. The conversation often included being happy and having good values. Whenever we talked about material possessions, things that some of my friends had that I really wanted, my grandmother always put her hand to her heart and then to mine and said, *"Ineweinik merste wichtik."* ("Inside most important.")

I think that she was trying to tell me that material things could be bought and sold, but inner peace and happiness could not. While I did not fully comprehend then what she was trying to impart to me, I do now. She wanted me to know that I needed to be true to myself and at peace with myself on the inside in order to maintain a life that would be full of satisfaction.

Shortly after I began my telephone support group for handicapped mothers and shut-ins, Comfort Call of Greater New Jersey, I really began to understand my grandmother's wisdom regarding spirituality. Once the calls increased in volume, I felt ill-equipped to handle their serious nature. I was without peace of mind and felt ill at ease. I did not know what to do, so I asked myself what my grandmother would say to me if she were there. I realized that she would probably tell me, *"Ineweinik merste wichtik."* ("Inside most important.")

And so I focused on that. I had always wanted to return to school, but my health had been a deterrent. I knew that my grandmother would encourage me to *tung* (take action). I believed that I would be at peace if I could undertake the challenge of college. And so I decided that I would go back to school and take only one class at a time. Friends would ask me why I was going to school when I was so ill. I would respond by saying, "Why not?" I realized that returning to university had nothing to do with what others thought. In the end, what mattered was what I thought about and what would make me happy internally.

I am so happy that I persevered, even in the face of great adversity. After my cardiac bypass surgery, my friends said, "Now you'll finally stop school!" My response was, "Not on your life!!!" My grandmother always gave me the feeling that life is what you make it and that material possessions are not as important as what is in one's heart. I believe that is very true. As an adult, I conduct interactive workshops for personal growth. One of the topics that I cover is spirituality, and I usually present that workshop at the end of a series of workshops because of its paramount importance.

What Grandma said:

Don't look to see what others have;
be grateful for what you have.

Don't try to act like a big shot; it
doesn't do you any good.

You've got to be happy with yourself.

Listen, there's always someone better
off than you; there are also some who
don't have as much as you do.

Don't be fooled by what somebody has.

Don't just look at the book's pretty cover;
see what's inside. That's what counts.

Don't only look in big boxes; you can
find nice things in small boxes.

What Grandma said:

Don't be like him; he brags a lot—be yourself.

Don't get too big for your britches. It's not pretty.

Know who you are inside.

Sometimes it's bigger than us.

Keep thinking good thoughts; look into your heart.

Try to figure out who you are.

Oy vay, I can't make you love yourself;
only you can do that.

Believe in yourself; I want you to do
it, but I can't make you do it.

Things come and go; hearts are important.

Memory:

The irony of this teaching lies more in the "do nots" versus the "dos." While my grandmother often told me what was beneficial to do, she also gave me lots of warnings about what not to do and what would not be in my best interest. As I sit here writing this book, I have tears in my eyes, because it was my grandmother who taught me life's lessons, and I am so grateful to her for that. My grandmother always said to me, "Kleg nischt a nar." ("Don't be a fool.") She led me to believe that there were enough people out there who would fool me and that I should not be one of them!

I remember having a birthday party when I was nine years old. I invited all of my close girlfriends. I was elated that the most popular girl in the class was attending. Knowing that my friends would be impressed made me feel special and important. My grandmother gave me a birthstone ring, a ruby, as a gift. It was exactly what I wanted; all of my friends had birthstone rings. It was my first piece of jewelry. I loved it so much. I put it on my finger to show everybody but then placed it back in the box for safekeeping. I then moved all of the presents into my bedroom. Shortly thereafter, my friends and I sang "Happy Birthday" and ate the cake. The atmosphere was electric and exciting. Wow! Receiving a ruby ring and having the most popular girl at school attend my birthday party made me truly ecstatic. After my friends left the party, I went into my bedroom to look more closely at my presents. When I looked into the black velvet box that contained my ruby ring, it was gone. I couldn't believe it. My mother told me that I must have misplaced it, but my grandmother taught me otherwise.

She said, "Der fingerl zayn nisht nor firn avek." ("The ring did not just walk away.") At first I didn't understand what she was trying to tell me. After I had a tantrum she let me know that the behavior would not make my ring suddenly appear. She then said to me, "Loz unz onrufn`du khavern zikh efsher zey *visn etvos."* ("Let's call your friends, because maybe they know something.") What could they know that I didn't? But since I loved my grandmother so much and knew that she wanted the best for me, I started telephoning my friends (and not on a cell phone ... who could have imagined!?)

All friends that I called seemed to respond in a peculiar manner; they kept changing the subject. When I returned to the subject of the ring, they all said that they had to hang up. I saw the look of concern on my grandmother's face but had not a clue as to what was going on. My grandmother told me to call my closest friend back, a girl I had known for many years. On my second call to her, she began to cry. I was completely baffled by then. She ultimately told me that that the popular girl had stolen my ring. I could not believe it but had no doubt that she was telling the truth. To make a long story short, the popular guest finally admitted to me that she had, in fact, stolen my ring. She was not even apologetic. As a matter of fact, she acted quite indignant.

My grandmother then taught me about what is important in life. It's not a ring or having the most popular girl at school at your birthday party. What is important is not something outside of yourself; it is what is inside that is important. She taught me not to base who I am on other things or people. As noted above, for this category of learning my grandmother taught me more about the "don'ts" of life than the "dos." She taught me not to have a false sense of self, and not to define myself by what I had or what I wanted to have.

After I discovered the thief, my grandmother said the most profound words to me: *"Nischt here schmok, mer wichtik in ineweinik, zach kumn geindon, nit barimen sich, nit imponirn."* ("Don't be fooled by others. Inside is most important. Do not brag or be impressed.") She taught me to be true to myself, to have my own values and belief systems and to follow them so I would be comfortable and fulfilled on the inside.

Her words taught me to seek and find a deep sense of myself in order to lose my fears and gain inner peace. Above all, I learned that inner peace and serenity do not depend upon social status, possessions, recognition, or approval from others. We become happier and more liberated individuals when we find our own individual peace of mind and heart.

Self and Others

While we strive to have our own needs met, we must not forget that we live in a social world. We interact with others; our lives are interdependent and often interconnected. It is important to think of others and be considerate of them. We must not think only of ourselves. While we must think of others, we must remain cognizant of our own needs so that we do not give away too much of ourselves to others.

When I was a child I always wanted to be liked, so I tried to please everybody. At one of my birthday parties, I gave pieces of cake to all my friends to take home. When there was one piece of cake left, I looked around to see if I could give the last piece to someone. Before I did so, my grandmother whispered in my ear, *"Sein fain in anderer ober nit gebn anz ich-gufe."* ("Be nice to others, but do not give them your whole self.") I didn't really understand that until much later in life.

Even as a young adult, I always tried to be kind to others and to please them. Whenever a friend wanted to go to a movie, I always acquiesced to what she wanted. One night, a particular friend selected a movie that I had already seen. When I told her that I had seen the movie and perhaps we could select another movie, she became furious and told me to go home because she was seeing the movie that she wanted to see.

Only then did my grandmother's teachings make sense to me. I realized that, as a people-pleaser, I always tried to accommodate everybody else, even to my own detriment. I also realized that even if we try to please others all of the time, it will not always work out well. I ultimately understood that I was giving away so many pieces of myself that I no longer knew who I was or what I wanted. And so, I stopped being a people-pleaser. While I was always kind and pleasant; I also identified my own needs that had to be met in order to preserve the different components of Dr. Sheila.

When I conduct a personal growth workshop series now, I always incorporate a concept of *self and others* into my lectures. I label this particular lecture, "Who am I?" Since my grandmother helped to teach me who I am, I am always cognizant of what others ask of me. While I am accommodating, if I really do not want to do something that is asked of me, I will not do it. However, I will be sure to tell others who do want to do it, "Enjoy, enjoy, enjoy!" Thanks, Bubbie.

What Grandma said:

Don't slam the door.

Keep the music down.

It's so loud, I can't think; turn down that television.

Be on time; people hate waiting.

Listen, don't just think of yourself.

Call me if you're going to be late because I'll worry.

Don't kick sand in people's faces
when you're at the beach.

Don't just open the bathroom door if it's closed; knock first. Somebody may be in there doing their business!

What Grandma said:

Hey, put that phone down; don't
listen in on their conversation.

Don't even think of talking back!

Don't curse at anybody; it's not nice!

You don't have to do everything he
does, if you don't want to.

You know, you don't always have to say yes to her.

Look, if you really don't want to do it, just say no.

Oy vay, when are you going to
start thinking about you?

Don't just follow what somebody else is
doing. It might be no good for you.

Memory:

I guess I passed my grandmother's teachings along to my daughter. When she was about ten years old, she was invited to a birthday party that was supposed to be "the party of the year." She bought a new dress and was very excited. The night before the party, she looked so sad that I asked her what was wrong. She said, "My friend Merry's dog just died, and I am not going to the party. I am going to stay with her." When we talked about this in greater depth, she said, "I wouldn't feel very good inside if I was not there for Merry when she is so lost and sad. But I am going to the breakfast tomorrow, and Merry will come with me, so I feel good about it." My daughter had figured out a way to be kind to her friend but to also take care of herself by attending the breakfast. What a good balance! I looked up into the sky and said a big "thank you" to my grandmother.

Anger

"Anger is a weed; hate is the tree" (St. Augustine). Everybody gets angry at some point. That's just the way life is. Anger is often sparked by a threat or an injustice. Anger is a normal human emotion that in and of itself is not a bad thing. It may even lead to growth and personal development. Anger often results in blaming others, feeling hurt, and using unkind language. But that is not what my grandmother taught me. I am not saying that she did not become angry; she did. But the manner in which she handled it seemed to be healthy.

Even though she never raised her voice to me, I always knew when my grandmother was angry. She did not name call or yell or blame. Being angry was just one part of life for her. It wasn't bad or good; it was just a normal component of everyday life. Whenever she sat down and called me by name, saying, *"Neitik redn"* ("Necessary to talk"), I knew that I was being held accountable for something she didn't like.

One day after school, my grandmother was angry at me because I had yelled at my mother. She made a glass of tea and told me, *"Far vos geschrei, redn woil gut, nebechdik."* ("Why are you yelling? Speak nicely is better—apologize!") She was trying to tell me that yelling did not serve any purpose. She encouraged me to apologize to my mother and tell her exactly what made me yell. I apologized to my mother and explained that I was angry because she had not listened to a story that I was trying to tell her about my day at school. Surprisingly, she listened attentively and then gave me a big hug, a rarity for her. I realized, at that very moment in time, that my psychic energy would be better spent explaining versus yelling.

To this day I always confront issues in an assertive manner and not in an aggressive manner. Whenever I become angry with a friend, I always remain very calm and verbalize that I am angry because I feel that some type of injustice has been done. I think that the way my grandmother handled anger was the reason that I became a mediator and received my PhD in conflict analysis and resolution. By the way,

I am always willing to apologize if I had misinterpreted the situation, which has happened upon occasion!

I am forever grateful that my grandmother taught me never to be afraid of anger. To this day, when I am angry with my husband and I tell him that it is necessary to talk, he knows what is to follow. While he does not really like confrontation, he doesn't become defensive any more because there is no blaming, just a discussion of feelings. The key is not to avoid anger but to handle it in a healthy and effective manner.

What Grandma said:

Think before you say something you might regret.

Don't be foolish; stop and think first. You'll make trouble.

Once it's out of your mouth you can't
take it back ... it's there forever.

You better not say that to him/her or
there will be trouble, big trouble.

Don't fly off the handle so fast!

Memory:

When I was about eleven years old I remember being angry at my brother for blasting his music. I was studying for a test and unable to concentrate. I remember telling my brother to turn down the music, to no avail. I came out of my bedroom stomping my feet and slamming my bedroom door. My grandmother intercepted me before I went into my brother's room to begin yelling at him and calling him unkind names. She said to me, "Denkn erscht nebechdik kenen." ("Think first; sorry, can't take it back.") She was trying to de-escalate my anger by making me stop and think about the repercussions of what I wanted to do. In essence, she was making me stop and count to ten so that my anger could be dealt with in a healthy and productive manner.

Family solidarity was very important to my grandmother, and she believed that siblings ought to respect each other. And so she was letting me know that I ought to stop and think before I blurted out something that I would later regret. To this day, when I feel that I might inappropriately say something in anger, I step on the heel of my shoe and pivot away until I am calmer. Dealing with anger at the height of one's fury is unproductive. Whenever I conduct workshops I always include the concept of anger. In and of itself, anger is not bad; how one deals with the anger is the tricky part.

What Grandma said:

Stop screaming; it doesn't do anybody any good.

Stop blaming him! Listen to yourself!!

Don't curse; it makes everything worse.

Keep counting; maybe more than twenty is good!

Don't get so hot around the collar.

Don't just blurt something right out. You better think first.

You can't think straight when you're yelling like that.

Calm down so we can talk about it.

It's not what you say, but how you say it.

Some things are better left unsaid, believe me.

Let's talk like two normal human beings.

Your blood pressure is going to explode, so calm down.

Who can talk to you when you're like this? Nobody, you hear? Nobody, even Grandma, as much as I love you.

Memory:

Until my husband retired he was a workaholic. I accepted that as part of my life. After doing a great deal of cooking for a party one night, I let the garbage pile up. Instead of emptying the garbage as I usually did, I started resenting the fact that he was working so much. I started to build up blame and anger before he even arrived home. I greeted him at the door and started screaming like a crazed individual.

My husband looked shell-shocked and bewildered. I remember my grandmother saying to me, "Wer kenen hern men kopweitik?" ("You're giving me a big headache; who will even listen to you when you are like this?). I remember the same look of bewilderment on my grandmother's face when I yelled as a child. I stopped and laughed, which baffled my husband even more. I told him that my grandmother would not like my behavior and neither did I. I apologized, and we had fun making up. By the way, I took out the garbage myself!

Conflict Resolution

Conflict, a normal response to a perceived injustice, is inevitable! My grandmother taught me that conflict, if not handled appropriately, saps one's strength and energy. Too often, individuals focus on being angry and blaming each other. They often forget to focus on the situation itself. I remember being very angry with my teacher for having given me a bad grade. I was focused on the teacher and not on the situation. I cried and cried and cried, and I yelled at my teacher, even though she was not in my house. When my eyes were swollen and red and I could no longer speak because of the laryngitis I developed from screaming so much, my grandmother sat down at the table with me.

She said the following words to me, *"Oisbrengn energie teier."* ("Wasted energy, and at such a high cost.") She was trying to tell me that it was a waste of my time and energy to focus on the person without examining the problem. She encouraged me to calmly and reasonably talk to the teacher about the issue at hand and to explain my side of the situation. I did so, and the teacher heard what I had to say and changed my grade. After the incident, my grandmother told me, *"Kukn problem nit menschen, seir gut."* ("Look at problem, not the people, good.") She was wise beyond her years because this concept is an intergral component in mediation and conflict resolution.

Whenever I present a professional workshop, I always have individuals participate in a role play in which one participant uses judgmental words (*good, bad, always, never, right, wrong, should, shouldn't*.) The scenario helps the audience to understand how a conflict may be sparked. The individual being judged invariably becomes defensive. The conflict then escalates. Each person blames the other; respective positions remain steadfast.

After the individuals understand how conflict is triggered, they then participate in additional conflict resolution role playing. They learn to: separate people from the problem; seek commonalities and alternate solutions; select and implement the best solution considered; and evaluate the outcome.

In my personal life, I have tried to help people in my gated community with conflict resolutions. Residents began to recommend me to each other as a conflict resolution specialist. Because of my track record, I was elected to the board of directors and have served on that board for nine years as a certified mediation specialist.

I always tell the participants that I will not be able to guarantee that the resolution will be exactly as they hope. I do, however, guarantee that I will listen attentively to them and do the best I can to help them resolve the issue that concerns them both. That generally acts as an ice breaker because each individual feels both heard and validated.

I try to impress upon individuals that negative energy is a waste of one's precious time. I recommend that they use psychic energy for more creative endeavors. I encourage individuals not to be afraid of conflict but to beware of the negative energy associated with blaming individuals versus dealing with the disputed issue at hand.

Since people are inherently different, it's normal for conflict to arise when two or more people come together. Because each individual is unique and responds to situations in a reflexive and subjective manner, multiple realities exist. While many individuals view conflict as negative, it may actually be positive in terms of making changes. The manner in which conflict is handled is the key. If individuals are able to express their feelings honestly, listen attentively, remain assertive, and collaborate effectively, there is potential for growth and enhanced relationships.

If we think of conflict as bringing to light those differences that exist, we can more easily view it as an opportunity to maximize all of the potential outcomes of the problem at hand. Through the use of an effective conflict resolution process, individuals can explore their conflicting differences and may then be able to develop a more open and honest process of relating to each other.

I encourage all of my participants to focus, not on the people involved, but rather on the specific issue in question. Once my clients move away from blaming each other and instead identify a problem that needs to be addressed, the energy shifts from negative to positive. This enables further positive interaction to occur, because both parties are searching for a collaborative solution that will be mutually acceptable.

What Grandma said:

Don't run away; stay and face whatever it is.

Talk to me—don't sulk!

I'm not a mind reader; tell me what you are thinking.

It can't be just what you want; it has to be what you both want.

There's no rush; stop and think first.

Ask somebody else's opinion; two heads are better than one.

You can't fight fire with fire.

Monkey see, monkey do … stop that!

Listen to what she is saying; stop judging her.

Stop being so stubborn. There may be something you didn't think about.

What Grandma said:

Be quiet and listen.

Listen, you're getting no place fast; let me sit down
with both of you so we can straighten this thing out!

If you don't have anything good to
say, keep your mouth closed!

Take a look at yourself; stop blaming everybody else!

Don't keep yelling, it does nobody any good.

Give the guy a chance to tell his side of the story.

Don't get so excited.

You can't think straight when you're yelling like that.

Calm down so we can talk about it; I'm
not talking when you are this crazy.

Memory:

When I was about ten years old, a girlfriend came over to my house. We were going to play with our dolls. I allowed my friend to play with my doll, but when my turn came to play with her doll, she would not allow me to do so. I remember locking her outside of my bedroom and telling her to go home. I remained in my room crying while my friend cried in the hallway outside of my room. My grandmother heard all of the crying, and she brought my friend into my room.

She sat on my bed and said, "Narischkeit, geschrein opfal." ("Foolishness, wasted energy.") In her broken English, she asked us what the problem was. We determined that it involved the length of play we each had with the dolls. My grandmother went into the kitchen, got the timer, and set it to ten minutes. I never understood how she did that! As she was leaving my room she said, "Schpiln, nischt geschrein beser harz." ("Play, don't cry; it's better for the heart.") She was trying to help us realize that blaming each other was a waste of energy. She examined the problem, gave us each a time limit, and converted our energy to positive ... to playing with the dolls!

Since I am not a well person, I realize just how precious one's energy can be for one's overall well-being. And so I try to preserve my energy and use it in a positive fashion; negative energy simply saps one's strength!

Boundaries

Sometimes we are afraid that others might not like us, so we are afraid of saying "no" to them. While you may choose to engage in obligations and situations that you are not thrilled about, it is not okay to say "yes" too many times when you really do not want to do something. When we give away too much of ourselves, we have a hard time finding the "me." This situation may cause inner conflict. Whenever I was in a quandary and on the verge of taking on too many tasks, my grandmother would invariably say to me, *"Dich gut person, passik nit zogn."* ("You are a good person, and it is acceptable to say no.")

Saying "no" is one of the most difficult challenges that my clients face. When I teach about boundaries in my workshops, people often say to me, "I can't say 'no' because it means that I am selfish." My reply is that it is self-caring, not selfish. If each one of us is not willing to take care of himself or herself, then who will? I think of it this way: I am a caring person but if I say "yes" when I really want to say "no," I end up in conflict with myself. One of the biggest stressors for my clients is their fear of saying "no" to others. They are afraid that the other individual will be angry at them.

As an adult, I am asked to participate on boards of directors for a variety of organizations. I always pause first, evaluate the time involved, and ask myself, "If I do this, will I become stressed and angry at myself?" If the answer is "yes," I listen to my grandmother's words of wisdom and tell them that I am flattered to be asked but that I really do not have sufficient time available to carry out the tasks successfully. Nobody seems to take offense, and I am happy with myself! If we give away too much of ourselves to others, we do not have enough left for us!

What Grandma said:

You already saw that movie twice, why are you
going again just because she wants to?

You keep running there every day,
don't you ever get sick of it?

How can you keep saying "yes" to him all the time?

What about you, what about what you want?

There you go again! What's the matter with you?

So, when is "enough enough!"

You're crazy, you are running yourself
ragged ... and for what!

For crying out loud, just tell her that you
can't do it, it's gonna be okay!

You don't have a minute's peace for yourself.

What's it gonna take for you to stop
running yourself ragged?

I don't understand why you just can't tell him "no."

Memory:

When I was about ten years old I was very excited because both of my friends were having birthday parties, but on the same day. I didn't know which party to attend, so I said "yes" to both of them. I didn't want the girls to be mad at me. I became more and more nervous as the day approached. Increasing my stress level, I told each girl that I would come to her house on the morning of the party to help decorate with balloons and to make the goody bags. I became so upset that I started to cry. (Boy, did I do a lot of crying as a kid!) My grandmother heard me crying and, once again, came to my rescue.

She asked me the following question: "Zwei plaz selbik, meshuge, narischeit?" ("Two places, same time? Crazy foolishness.") She asked me how I planned to be in two places at the same time. I was not able to give her a logical answer. We discussed how I could call my friends, tell them the truth, and divide my time so that it was comfortable for me, not for them. She helped me to devise a plan whereby I would spend preparation time and one hour at the first party.

From there I would go directly to the second party for another hour. I was able to attend both parties and be honest with my friends, as well as with myself. Above all, I remained comfortable with myself. After my Grandma helped me with the arrangements, she said the following profound words, "Woos men great kulak baser, went as is nitric zoo." ("It's about what you are willing to do; sometimes it is necessary to say no.") In the end, my friends were happy, and I was happy. My grandmother helped me to realize that saying no was not a bad thing ... and was even necessary in some situations. Even today, if I am tempted to say yes when I really want to say no, my heart starts to pound, and I think of my grandmother's lesson!

Solving Problems and Making Decisions

Some decisions are simple and routine. Others require more time and attention. Those latter decisions are akin to problem solving, which is a serious matter. Solving problems takes time. It is a process that involves identifying the issue, thinking of alternative solutions, weighing the consequences of those solutions, selecting the best solution available, carrying out the solution, and evaluating what you have done. Asking "what if?" and "what then?" questions along the way will be helpful.

When I was in grade school I had to do a project for school. I kept focusing on how I would do the project. Would I color, paint, use clay, or draw? My grandmother said, *"Wos ton machn?"* ("So what are you going to do it on?") I hadn't even thought about that. She asked me how I could make plans if I did not even know the specific project that I wanted to undertake. Ergo, identifying the problem.

I decided to do my project on Betsy Ross and the American flag. I was ready to start drawing on the piece of paper when my grandmother said, *"Nischt schnel, wos hois?"* ("Not so fast—what supplies do we have in the house?") We searched all of the cabinets in the house and found some red fabric. I now had the option of drawing the flag or using the red fabric. Ergo, think of alternative solutions.

I asked myself how the project would look if I colored the flag instead of making the flag out of fabric. I realized that if I colored the flag, there would not be as much variety in the project. Ergo, weighing the consequences of each solution. So I selected the fabric alternative for making the flag because it made a great deal of visual impact. Ergo, carrying out the solution.

Lastly, I looked at my project and was happy that I had made the choices that I had. Ergo, evaluating the solution. My grandmother helped me every step of the way, even though she couldn't see the materials. She kept saying, *"Asoi het, asoi gut."* ("So far, so good.") She taught me that problem solving was a serious endeavor that took a great deal of time because it involved many components. It also required cognitive skills and patience.

I also realized that having ideas and help from another individual could be very beneficial. Even today, I welcome feedback and constructive criticism because I realize that I do not know what I do not know. Whenever I want to rush into something, I always hear my grandmother's words in the background: *"Nit schnel, ophaltn, denkn, planewn."* ("Not so fast—stop, think, and plan.") Her words have also helped me in my professional life.

As an undergraduate college student, I was hired to help college students acclimate to university life. The focus of the tutoring revolved around problem solving and decision making. I tried to encourage the students to budget their time wisely and to use forethought. I always began by telling them how my own grandmother had prepared me for college while I was still a little girl. I often quoted her words to them: *"Ophaltn, denkn, planewn."* ("Stop, think, and plan first.") The students often converted the Yiddish words to the following English words: "Office, den, and plane."

Many of the students initially arrived at the tutoring session without even a notebook, pen, or pencil. After they heard my grandmother's words often enough, I often overheard them say to each other, "You didn't forget the office, den, or plane, did you?" The students learned that problem solving and decision making were serious and time-consuming endeavors. My grandmother's words lived on. Thank you, Bubbie!

What Grandma said:

So what exactly is the problem?

Listen, let me help you.

Don't just walk away; let's sit down and think this out.

Let's look at maybe what we can do.

Maybe I have an idea you didn't think of.

Let's try this one; if it doesn't work,
we'll try something else.

Sometimes you have to try, try, and try again.

There's always a way out; you just
have to think about it more.

Listen, don't give up; think about
how you can solve this thing.

I'm willing to help you with this but
I can't do it without you.

Sit down; this is going to take awhile.

What Grandma said:

All talk is just a waste of time if you don't do anything.

Don't just ignore this; it won't go away.

Don't make light of this; it's a real problem.

Don't make it bigger than it is.

Hey, this is your problem and not his!

Maybe if my head works with your head, we'll come up with something.

Think things through. Please!

If you don't know what the exact problem is, you can't fix it.

What sense does it make to just talk about it?

You better think about what you are going to do before you do it.

What Grandma said:

So, what do you think is the best thing to do?

Let others help you if you aren't sure what to do.

Don't make quick complications or judgments;
you need to know all the facts.

Stop, too confusing; make simple.

In the end it's really up to you, so take your time.

If you pick something to do and it doesn't work, you'll
go back and pick something else. That's all there is to it!

Screaming at each other won't
help you solve the problem.

Pay attention to details.

Don't think about that yet; you'll cross
that bridge when you come to it.

Try to be more organized.

Memory:

I was getting ready to go to my first dance at school. All my friends were very excited. The topic of conversation focused on the outfits that we would wear. I started to try on what I thought would be appropriate but decided that all of my possibilities were terrible. I started throwing different articles of clothing on the floor. My grandmother had very keen hearing, and she heard the hangers clicking against the floor. She came into the room, sat down on my bed, and felt all of the clothes lying on the floor. She told me to pick them up and very calmly said, "Opschtal energie, nuscgt nirgbgaubt." ("Stop wasting energy; if not today, tomorrow.") I think that her intention was to let me know that tomorrow was a new day that provided more time for action and creativity.

My grandmother taught me that rushing to judgment was unproductive. She told me that if I became calm and rational I would be able to make better decisions for myself. And so, I stopped complaining and picked up the clothes. She then said, "Nit denkn geschrei, beser mit morch." ("Don't think by yelling; it's better with the brain.") Her words made so much sense to me. Instead of complaining I sorted out the skirts and the blouses. I then matched the colors to see which coordinated well together. My grandmother brought me some of her scarves to try. After about an hour of evaluating each choice, I made my final decision, and I was happy. I learned that to make a wise decision, one must take the necessary time to think about the total situation. For without forethought, there is chaos and no solution.

Preparation, Thinking Ahead, and Setting Goals

Preparation means thinking ahead and planning. Doing things without forethought may create future problems, as I learned from my grandmother. When I was a little girl, I always tried to do well in school. I handed in assignments on time and studied for exams well before the date of the test. I guess I had always listened to my grandmother's advice: *"Nischt denk zore."* ("If you don't plan ahead you will get into trouble.")

When I was about eleven years old, I had a research paper due. One of my friends was having a birthday party the night before the paper was due. I convinced my parents to allow me to attend the party, even though it was on a school night. I came home very late and was too tired to proofread my paper. Instead of getting an A on my paper, I received a lower grade because of the spelling errors and incorrect grammar and punctuation. I realized that by not listening to my grandmother's advice, I fell into the trap. I did not plan ahead and budget my time well, so I had to pay the consequences. From that point on I always had my papers ready one week in advance of the due date.

When I first returned to college as an adult, I was excited. My overall goal was to achieve a degree in social work so that I could better serve the hotline that I had established for handicapped mothers and shut-ins. My poor health prevented me from attending school on a full-time basis. And even though I was disappointed, I knew that I had to be realistic. So my short-term goal became taking one or two classes at a time.

I was excited and did my best to learn and think critically. It took me fourteen years to achieve my BSW. Once I realized that I could accomplish that goal, I moved onto my next goal: achieving an MSW, which I did. I was able to gain entrance to a university in Florida as an advance standing student. This meant that I had to attend school for one year on a full-time basis. The one issue that proved problematic was that the university for the MSW was located in a different state, a state in which I owned a residence.

My husband and I discussed the issue at great length. We decided that I would live in the out-of-state residence and attend school on a full-time basis. I was nervous, but I knew that I could do it. I remember hearing my grandmother's words of encouragement in my ear: *"Gein, gein, meglech derschrokn, bisl firn a sach."* ("Keep going, don't be afraid; anything is possible, and a little can lead to a lot.") She was trying to tell me that anything was possible as long as it was realistic. She also helped me to understand that by setting short- and long-term goals, I would be able to achieve things incrementally.

After one year at the university my family, including grandchildren, came to my graduation carrying balloons that said, "Way to go, Grandma!" Another goal accomplished. But that was only part of my plan.

When I decided to seek my final long-term goal, earning a PhD, I thought it over very carefully. When my daughter gave me a bookmark that said, "One day at a time, baby steps will get you there," I knew that I was on my way.

My dream started to become a reality after I enrolled in Nova Southeastern University for a PhD. After eight years of hard, hard work, I am now known as Dr. Grandma to my grandchildren and Dr. Sheila to others. My whole family attended my dissertation defense. My grandchildren looked at me with awe as I explained many things that they did not understand. Thank goodness my granddaughter Isa was there to help with last-minute technical glitches. I had achieved Nirvana.

My grandmother taught me that *"Plan, meglach neitik."* ("Anything is possible as long as you have a plan, a goal.") Goals must be realistic and achievable. Achieving short-term goals provides the impetus to move forward with long-term goals. I was able to set realistic goals and break them down into small, manageable tasks. Each time I was successful I felt good about myself and created the drive and stamina to keep moving ahead.

My children also benefited from my grandmother's wisdom. My daughter wanted to earn her doctorate in pharmacy, and my son wanted to have multiple businesses as an entrepreneur. Both have accomplished their goals and are as proud of me as I am of them!

What Grandma said:

You need to be able to walk before you can run.

Don't put everything in only one place.

It might rain so take an umbrella.

Looks like snow, take your boots.

Don't forget to take your wallet; you'll be in big trouble.

Memory:

My grandmother always told my brother and me, "Men kein mol nit, gelt." ("You never know—plan ahead, take money.") I heard her say those words over and over, especially to my brother, who had a driver's license. One particular night my brother went out with his friends, and he did not take any money with him. He and his friends got lost and were unable to make a telephone call to a parent. As a result, they slept in the car overnight. My parents were furious and worried. Finally, my brother arrived home the next morning.

After that incident I realized how important it was to think ahead and to ask the following question: "What if?" And so I made sure that my children always had money in case of an emergency. Due to today's technology, my grandchildren have cell phones in case of emergency! I wonder what my grandmother would think about that!

What Grandma said:

Don't just do it; you've gotta stop and
think first. It's crazy, oh no!

Don't spend all your money; save some,
or you might end up with none.

Think about it some more, because
you got to watch the dollar.

Study if you want to go to college; college
is for smart people to get smarter.

If you don't understand something, ask the teacher.

You better ask your father first.

Oy vay, you can't just do something like that!

Don't forget to take your lunch or you'll be hungry.

Don't forget to put the mat down
in the tub so you won't slip.

Put on clean underwear; you might
get into an accident.

What Grandma said:

Decide what you need to do first!

Doing things without thinking first
could lead you to big trouble.

Don't drive fast; you could get into an accident.

Before you go across the street, look
to make sure there are no cars.

Don't ever swim alone; you never
know what could happen.

Always save for a rainy day; you never
know what life will bring.

Practice your spelling words so you
can win the spelling bee.

Eat your breakfast—you can't learn so
good without food in your stomach.

Memory:

When I was a teenager all of my friends began to drive. We were so excited. One night a big party was scheduled. All of the students were going. One of the boys who was considered to be very wild asked me and my friends to go with him. All of my friends said that they would go with him. When I told my grandmother that I was going with my friends, she asked me what kind of driver the young man was. Even though I knew he was wild, I told her that he was a careful driver. Unfortunately, my grandmother knew the boy's grandmother, who was worried that her grandson was not a cautious driver.

She said, "Emozie tirche, opschtal denkin, welcher zufal." ("Don't go from emotion; stop and think first about consequences, an accident.") My parents drove me to the party while my friends went with the young man. They had a car accident; luckily nobody was permanently injured.

And so my grandmother taught me that we must learn to respond to situations not with just a weak, emotional, knee-jerk reaction but rather from a rational position of strength. Taking action without forethought can certainly lead to disastrous results. Today, I try to use reason over emotion.

Anxiety and Coping Mechanisms

"A crust eaten in peace is better than a banquet partaken in anxiety"—Aesop

Webster's Dictionary defines anxiety as a state of mind in which one is troubled and distressed. Life is full of daily challenges, some small, some large. It's not how many challenges one has but rather how one deals with those challenges. My grandmother helped me to understand that when I was nervous and my mind was racing, I would not be able to access and utilize my optimal coping mechanisms and problem-solving skills.

I remember the first time I had a date. I was so excited and nervous that I could hardly think. My date told me to think about what I would like to do. I just sat on my bed saying, "I can't do this. I can't do this!" As the night progressed, I had made no decision because I remained inert and unfocused.

My grandmother recognized that my normal coping mechanisms were defunct. So she said, *"Du nischt kenkin gang gut beser."* ("You can't get anywhere when you're like this. Let's go for a walk.") Once I calmed down I was able to think straight and problem solve. I decided on a movie in case my date might be boring!

My grandmother was trying to tell me that if I was anxious and highly emotional, I would not be able to make appropriate and informed decisions about anything in my life. She helped me to understand that taking time to calm oneself down first is essential. Even today, when I feel my pulse racing or fists clenching, I become aware of my anxiety and access my grandmother's wisdom. To calm down, I usually listen to one Frank Sinatra song, which then enables me to continue my decision making in a rational manner.

We must each find our own mechanism that that will provide a calming effect. Anxiety prevents an individual from high functioning and straight thinking—qualities that are necessary in today's hectic, challenging world.

What Grandma said:

Don't get so nervous; we'll work it out.

If you stop walking back and forth and
sit down, we can talk about it.

You're so upset, let Grandma help you.

Stop shaking your foot and let's talk.

It won't help to worry; let's try to
better figure out what to do.

Stop wringing your hands.

Relax, slow down.

You're too upset now; let's talk about it later.

If you keep walking in circles, how will
we ever figure out what to do first? And
believe me, you will get dizzy too.

Listen, calm down. Let's go bake some
cookies, and you'll feel better.

Don't bite off more than you can chew. You will choke!

What Grandma said:

Better to do it later when you feel better, not now.

You want to make the solution or stay with the problem?

Slow down; I can tell you're getting nervous.

Don't be too hasty.

Crying alone never solved anything.

You can't think when you're so excited.

Calm down, eat a cookie.

Relax, have some chicken soup; *"Michel!"* ("Delicious!")

Take it easy. Take it easy, you hear me?

Oy, don't cry! Grandma will fix it and make it better.

Eat, you'll feel better.

Don't let every little thing bother you.

No chopped liver for you; it'll make you feel worse.

Memory:

When I was about twelve years old I forgot to bring home a school book that was necessary to study for an exam. I kept shaking my foot back and forth, so my grandmother asked me what was wrong. I still am amazed that she knew that I was moving my foot. I guess she heard my foot kicking against the leg on the chair. I told her that I didn't want to talk about it. She asked me if shaking my foot was the answer to my apparent problem.

I laughed and acknowledged that she was accurate in her assessment. Just being upset was not going to solve my problem. She finally said to me, "Darfen sgule, nischt ander." ("We need a solution, not another problem.") She made me realize that anxiety was an additional weight on my shoulders. She made me realize that I could have one problem or two problems.

One problem was to deal only with accessing the schoolbook; the other would include dealing with anxiety as well as with the schoolbook. I had the ability to decide if I would remain part of the problem ... or instead focus on a solution. I selected the latter. Further discussion revealed the possibility of my mother driving me to school to pick up the book. It seemed like a good solution, so I asked my mom and she said, "Yes!" I was pleasantly surprised because her normal response would have been to blame me for forgetting the book in the first place!

And so, today I always ask myself if I want one or two problems. I always select one problem, because it inevitably leads to a solution, not an additional problem.

Assertiveness

Many individuals believe that being assertive is a negative quality. Quite the contrary! Many mistakenly equate aggressiveness with assertiveness. Aggressiveness brings out the "bully" in us, but assertiveness helps us to clearly define our needs with reason, not emotion. Assertiveness allows us to express our needs in order to have them met. Assertiveness is a very good quality to possess!

I was very shy as a child and reluctant to ask for what I wanted or needed. When my grandmother sensed that I was reticent to speak up, she always said the following, *"Nischt einwendn!"* ("I am not a mind reader!") Whenever I sensed that my own children were reluctant to ask me for something, I always use my grandmother's Yiddish expression. Invariably my children would say, "Yeah, yeah, you don't read minds." Then they would tell me what they wanted to say.

Often when I do a family therapy session, family members, particularly children, are afraid to say anything negative about their home life. I encourage them to speak up, because if nobody knows what the issue is, it can never be resolved. I make the children understand that while I am in the room, sharing happens in a safe environment. The more they share in my office, the easier assertiveness will become and the sooner they will have their needs met.

Before children leave my office I repeat with them, three times, the following words, "My mom and dad are not mind readers!" It generally works out well for all.

What Grandma said:

Just tell me what you want; talk to me already!

Who knows what you're thinking? Not me.

I can't help you if you don't talk to me.

I'm here and I'm listening. Well??

Listen, it's up to you to speak up if you want something.

Don't threaten me. Just tell me nicely what you want.

How am I supposed to know what you want? Speak up.

Listen, you don't have to scream at me.

I'll listen better if you stop yelling at me; I'm not deaf.

Look, you'll get more bees with honey.

Don't be afraid to speak up. Maybe you will get what you want ... maybe not.

Just tell me already. I don't read the mind!

Memory:

When I was eleven years old I was having a birthday party at my house. I desperately wanted to have a special doll cake that I had seen in a bakery. The skirt of the doll was the cake itself. I went with my mother and grandmother to order a cake at a local bakery. They clerk presented me with a variety of possibilities but not the one that I really wanted. I rejected all of the possibilities but was afraid to tell my mother what I really preferred.

Each time I was asked the question regarding a final selection, I began my sentence with "Um, um." Apparently my grandmother sensed that there was something that I wanted to say. Finally she said to me, "Deiden zogn, mir nischt krgn weln." ("If you don't speak up, you'll never get what you want.")

So I spoke up, and to my delight my mother ordered the cake that I wanted. I have often encouraged my children to state their wants and preferences. While they realize that none of us can always have what we want or prefer, we will not know until we ask. As an adult, I always express my wants and preferences without aggressiveness, but with assertiveness. Sometimes I get what I want; other times I do not. That's life!

Fear

One of the strongest emotions that prevents us from moving toward self-actualization is our own fear. Fear can be paralyzing. When I first got sick as an adult, I was afraid that I would never be able to function again. I felt so isolated and alone because I was only in my thirties. I saw the world moving ahead while I stayed behind. I remembered my grandmother's words that she always used whenever I was frightened of a new endeavor upon which I was embarking, *"As men derschroken sich helfn."* ("If you are afraid, your *own selves* will help you.")

She was telling me not to be afraid and to have confidence in myself. She also said, *"Derschroken opfal lebedik oisfirn."* ("Fear stops living and accomplishing.") I remembered her words, overcame my fear, and created a support group for handicapped mothers, a social network not only for me but for others in the same situation.

I learned that fear keeps us "stuck" and prevents us from moving forward in order to satisfy our needs, expectations, and goals. I also understood that if I used my grandmother's "me, myself, and I" theory, I would be strong enough to face my fears through use of this comforting, unified approach.

What Grandma said:

I'm here, I'll catch you if you fall.

It's only a scratch; get back on the bike

Accident's can happen; get in
the car and keep driving.

Face challenges head on.

Don't be afraid, it's okay.

Be brave and strong.

It's just shadows on the wall. I'll make with
my hands a rabbit to show you.

You don't have to be afraid of the
dark … I'll leave a small light on.

Being afraid stops you from doing
things; so, don't be afraid.

What Grandma said:

Don't be afraid to raise your hand in school.

So what if you get the wrong answer? At least you tried.

Don't be afraid to drive; just stay in
your own lane—don't wander.

Don't be afraid. Grandma's here.

No monsters under this bed, only
dust. Dust can't hurt you.

Don't ever creep up behind me like that;
you almost scared me to death!

Go ahead, try it; it tastes good.

It's okay to try new things.

Grandma will protect you; don't be scared.

Don't be afraid; it's a costume with
a man like Daddy inside.

Memory:

My mother and father went on a trip to New York every year. I was excited because I knew that my grandmother would be spending a great deal of time with me. One night there was a torrential rain storm, with thunder and lightning. I was so scared that I ran into my grandmother's bed. She quelled my fears, stayed with me for a while, and told me not to be afraid. She explained that some things are beyond our control, like the rain and the snow. She told me that when G-d laughs the sun comes out, and when He cries it rains. She said, "Here nischt kein mol nit derschroken. Opschtal mit fil du." ("Who can know everything? Nobody. Fear can stop life. Don't be afraid. Be with the many yous.") When the lightning stopped and the rain slowed down, my grandmother opened the front door of our house so that I could feel the raindrops and not be afraid of them.

What she was trying to tell me was that I would never understand everything that happens in life. But if I allowed my fear to take over it would paralyze and prevent me from reaching self-actualization. She wanted me to know that there were three dimensions to each individual: "the me, the myself, and the I". She taught me well.

So today, I always try to face my fears. One of the most frightening times of my life was the night before my open heart surgery. I was petrified, and though I did not have my grandmother by my side, I did hear her words in my ear, "Mol nit derschroken. Opschtal mit fil du." ("Don't be afraid. Be with the many yous.") So, I smiled and comforted myself with the knowledge that the "me, the myself, and the I" would overcome the challenge together.

I guess I taught both of my children not to be afraid of the unknown as well. My daughter traveled around the world by herself after she received her PhD. When I told her that it was a mother's nightmare to have her daughter wandering around the globe by herself she told me that she was not going to be alone. She said, "I am going to be with me, myself and I, just like you taught me!" My son went to boarding school in Europe and traveled every weekend to absorb the different cultures. On one of his excursions, he decided to bungie jump. I was very happy that I learned about his adventure after the fact, when I realized that his body was in one piece. When I asked him what possessed him to engage in that endeavor he said, "You and your grandmother did not want me to be afraid of anything!" Oh, well, that's life.

Sadness

We operate from two different venues: reason and emotion. Whether we realize it or not, we talk to ourselves the most. We construct our realities through framing our thoughts in a particular manner. These thoughts are both subjective and reflexive. We tend to think in terms of binaries. Without sadness we could not understand joy. According to the Buddhists, we are the masters of our thoughts and feelings. We have both the choice and ability to think in either a positive or negative vein.

Sadness is a very crucial feeling that we all experience from time to time. It is normal to feel "blue" sometimes. But the good thing about feelings is that they can change from sad to happy. We cannot make decisions, solve problems, or resolve conflict based on our feelings. Each of us owns our own feelings, and that is perfectly acceptable. *How* and *what* we do with those feelings is crucial. Sometimes we can master our thoughts and reframe them in a manner that propels us forward. However, if sadness does not go away and prevents optimal functioning, then we need to have professional help to get us back on track.

My grandmother always validated my sadness and never made me feel that it was bad or wrong. I remember going to a Sadie Hawkins dance at school. The girls were supposed to ask the boys to dance. The first boy I asked to dance refused; I was devastated and went into the bathroom to cry. I wasn't deterred, because my grandmother always encouraged me to persevere in the face of adversity. She always said, *"Klein umet passik for mer."* ("A little sadness is okay, but keep going.") She wanted me to be able to overcome obstacles. So I tried again.

The next boy that I asked to dance also refused me. By this point I was really agonized, and I cried in the bathroom until it was time for my father to pick me up to go home. I was hysterical when I got into the car. My father asked me what had happened, and when I told him how I felt he said, "Don't worry about it!" How could he be so insensitive? So I cried even more.

When I finally got into my house I went to my bedroom in hysterics, but my grandmother came to my rescue. She helped me to understand that we must use reason over emotion; otherwise we stay sad and remain stuck. She helped me to realize that it was not the end of the world and that life is full of disappointments.

When my daughter was a teenager and experienced the usual trials and tribulations about boys, I would always repeat my grandmother's words to her: *"Losn gut, ophaltn oder men grois umet."* ("It's okay to let it out, but stop or you will really have something to be sad about.") I always coupled her words with a big hug. What my grandmother taught me was that I needed to put my sadness in perspective in relation to its overall importance in my life. Grandma helped me when she said those words, and I apparently helped my daughter as well when I said those words.

What Grandma said:

You are just as good as they are.

Don't give them anything for to think about.

Cry, but don't let them make you cry.

Cheer up, tomorrow is another day.

Everybody has a bad day now and then.

Let's try to put on a happy face.

When you think there is no place to turn … think again.

Don't' be afraid. I'm here.

It'll take time, but we'll see what's going on.

What Grandma said:

Come; let Grandma wipe those tears
from your handsome face.

It's always dark in the night; the morning is light.

Try to have some dreams; they help.

Everything will look better in the
morning; now go to sleep.

A good cry will make you feel better. It's okay.

You look so sad, my poor baby.

A scraped knee gets better; wait and you'll see.

You've been sad for so long, maybe
the doctor helps us.

Memory:

When I was in third grade a new student from another state came to our school. She had a birthday party and did not invite me. While some of my group of friends had been invited, others were not. On the night of the party my mother allowed me to have a sleepover at my house so that my loser friends and I could get together. Our goal was to wallow in self-pity. We sat around the big wooden table in my kitchen and lamented over how we despised the new girl. We then began to analyze why each of us had not been invited. Invariably each of us looked for her own flaws.

After about a half hour of listening to us bash ourselves, my grandmother came into the kitchen with her glesel tei (glass of tea.) Whenever she came to me with a glass of tea in hand and sat down where I was, I knew that she would teach me another one of her life's lesson. My girlfriends loved her because she knew so much about us even though she was blind. She always seemed to know when we were doing something sneaky, like smoking in the bathroom. My friends could not believe that she had caught us. That one was a no brainer; I told my friends that she had no sight but did have a sense of smell!

At the kitchen table, my grandmother validated our sadness. Then she asked each of us whom we would invite to our respective birthday parties. We each had different people on the list. Though there was some commonality, the lists were definitely not the same. We began to realize that we would not always be included in every event that was occurring.

But more importantly, she helped us to realize that we also would not include everyone at our own personal important events. With that realization we each found renewed dignity and respect. We also realized that not everybody would like us and that we would not like everybody either. This was one of the most important lessons that she passed down to me. It also helped my self-esteem.

My grandmother went around the table and patted every one of us on the shoulder and then quietly left us alone. Her last words were, "Sei nischt kenen geschrei: nor dir machn dir geschrei." ("Only you can make you cry.") She was telling us that if we felt good about ourselves inside, it was the only thing that mattered. I remember that as if it were yesterday. My friends, in unison, said, "We wish we had a bubbie (grandma) like that!" After those words, a lone tear streamed down my cheek. As I write this I still feel the warm flow of that tear against my cheek.

Irrational Thinking and Thought-Stopping

When we react emotionally instead of responding with reason, we may engage in behaviors that are self-defeating and self-destructive. It is imperative to have a cognitive mechanism to raise our consciousness of the signals so we can "stop" the potential damage that might lie ahead.

I remember being invited to a roller skating party when I was about eight years old. My friend's mother came to pick me up, and I did not have all my equipment together. My friend came to the door because I was taking too long. I heard my mother telling me to be sure and take my knee pads. I was so excited and in such a rush to leave that I did not take the time to go into my closet to retrieve the knee pads. I threw my stuff into a plastic garbage bag from my wastebasket, even though I had a nice sack to carry all of my equipment.

I did notice that all of my friends had their knee pads with them, but I dismissed my not having them; I was a real good skater and I wouldn't fall down, I thought. I never looked at the larger picture: because there would be other people in the rink I might collide with them. Initially, the skating was fine. But in a split second, I was knocked to the floor by a male skater who was racing around the rink. He hit me from behind, and I fell and skidded along the hard wooden floor on my knees.

I started to yell and scream at the boy, using words that were not very lady-like. My knees were a mess, and I was bleeding profusely. My friends immediately took me to the first aid station. The nurse on duty immediately asked me why I wasn't wearing knee pads. I told her that I had been in too much of a rush to find them in my closet.

She chided me for my irresponsible behavior and told me that my bruises would have practically been nonexistent if I had worn knee pads. I dreaded going home to tell my mother. I knew that she would be angry that I had not taken her advice. Boy, was I right! In her inimitable style my mother said, "Good for you. I'm glad it happened to you because you did not listen to me!"

No sympathy, only anger, which I guess I deserved. But she just made me angry that she was angry instead of caring. Once again my grandmother came to do the nurturing that I so desperately needed at that very moment. She took off the bandages and felt the bruises.

She took me into the bathroom and washed the wounds carefully, applying Mercurochrome and heaping spoonfuls (yes, spoonfuls) of Vaseline gel, her cure for all ills, onto my knee. She told me to use my fingers to rub in the gel so that the entire wound would be covered. She recommended that I do it myself because I was better able to see the extent of the wound.

She then suggested that I have cookies and milk with her in the kitchen. As soon as I saw her make her glass of tea and sit down I knew that I had done something that she did not like. She helped me to understand that I had ignored the most important issue, my safety. Because I did not budget my time well, I became rushed. This caused me to lose sight of my first priority. My grandmother helped me to realize, and verbally acknowledge, that because I did not stop to think rationally amidst my excitement, I became my own worst enemy.

I finally realized that by not thinking clearly, I had actually thought irrationally. She said, *"Kumendik zeit men bakumin, plan beser oismeidn, finger nos opschtal men."* ("Next time you get so excited, put your finger to your nose to stop yourself.") What she was trying to tell me was that I couldn't just do things without thinking, because I could get into trouble. She taught me that I needed to be able to identify a trigger and then do something overt to actually make me stop and think more clearly, like placing my finger on my nose.

And so, when I clench my fists and my heart begins to pound fast, I realize that I am well on the path toward irrational thinking. So what do I do next? I put my right index finger to my nose, look up to the sky, and say, "Thanks, Bubbie."

What Grandma said:

You can't think straight when you're like that. Where is your sense?

Listen to me; stop being hasty—you're acting crazy.

With ideas like that you'll get into big trouble.

Stop saying you hate them; hate is no good.

Stop right now, sit down, and think.

Oy vay, where did that come from?

You're screaming so loud, you're not thinking straight.

How did you get to that?

Memory:

I was invited to a birthday party for one of my closest friends. My mother asked me to go shopping for a birthday present for her, but I declined. I told her that we decided not to give any more birthday gifts to each other. My mother just shook her head and asked if I was certain about my decision. I assured her that I was. My grandmother overheard the conversation and decided to have one of her own with me.

At first we just talked about what kinds of things we did at birthday parties: food, decorations, goodie bags. Then we went on to talk about the best thing that occurs at birthday parties. No doubt, I immediately told her that the presents were the most fun. My grandmother remained silent for a few minutes, though it seemed like hours. Finally she asked me why we decided to stop giving presents if it was considered to be such an important part of the event.

I really did not know what to say. I offered a lot of, "Um, well, ah," but not much substance. I guess my grandmother knew that I had some type of hidden agenda, which I did. To this day I don't understand why I always "spilled my guts" to my grandmother. It was as though she always gave me some kind of truth serum or lie detector test. I finally told her that I was going to give my friend a beautiful garnet ring that I had received for my own birthday. How smart was I? It was the ring that my grandmother had given me. She was so shocked! Her voice went up two octaves, which was not the norm for her, and she said, "Oy vay, fun feld links!" ("Oh my G-d, from the field to the left!")

She was trying to find out whatever possessed me to make that totally irrational decision. From our conversation, she ascertained that I was giving it to my friend because she really liked it and I wanted her to like me. We then discussed gift-giving and respect and how doing something without actually thinking about it was a really bad idea. I apologized to her. I realized that she was sad that I was giving away the precious gift that she had bought for me with part of her savings. I was sad too! I realized that acting without forethought actually made no sense and does not really work!

Defense Mechanisms

Sometimes we try to avoid dealing with issues that are painful or cause anxiety. According to Freud, we engage in this behavior because we use defense mechanisms. These unconscious psychological behaviors allow us to deny, and deal with, the real tough issues that we face. Defense mechanisms come in many forms, such as minimizing, justifying, rationalizing, blaming others, and using humor. These are diversions that allow us to avoid dealing with the actual root cause of an issue. We all use defense mechanisms, but the degree to which we utilize them is key.

My grandmother taught me to listen carefully to what others were saying. She also taught me to listen to my own self-talk. I have no idea how she had insight into this area of behaviors. Maybe she was in therapy in the Old Country! More likely, she possessed some kind of special radar that identified how many times individuals practiced the same behaviors.

If she saw someone in the family making light of an issue, always defending a decision or action in a positive light, making jokes all the time, or blaming others, she would bend her head down onto her chest and very softly utter the following words, *"Bakumn unter emes."* ("The real truth is under.")

Whenever I start to blame my husband for something instead of taking responsibility for myself, I always stop and remember Grandma's words regarding hidden truths. While I must admit that I usually recognize the defense mechanism I am using, I am not always ready to deal with the tough underlying issue at the time. But if I procrastinate, I do myself a great disservice. Then again, I am human and it's really okay!

What Grandma said:

Don't make a joke out of everything.

Don't make it out to be him when it's really you.

Don't make so little of that—it's really important.

Don't make it such a big thing.

Hey, he didn't do it; you did.

Don't blame him; think about the
part you played in this.

It's your fault, not his.

Stop making it a mountain—it's not that big.

Memory:

My older brother built a stereo for himself while he was in college. Daily, he used it to play his favorite records (no DVDs, iPods, or cell phones back then). He worshipped that piece of equipment and told me never to touch it because I might break it. One day when my brother was still at school, I decided to take my friends into his room to play music on his stereo. I manually placed the needle on the record to make it play. I did not realize that the arm of the needle connected with the record automatically. Because I was doing this task incorrectly, the needle skidded across the whole record and scratched it beyond repair. I was always afraid of my brother, so I did not say anything about it to him. Real bad idea!

When he realized what had happened he came to me and asked me about it. He was in such a rage that I was petrified to tell him the truth. So I told him that I knew nothing about it and started getting angry at him for being angry at me. My grandmother overheard this scene. She said that she could tell by the hesitation between my words that I was not telling the truth. She made a glass of tea and sat at our kitchen table. I immediately knew that I had done something wrong. But I knew that my grandmother would not scream at me, so I sat down, ready to listen to her words of wisdom.

We talked about what had happened. She focused especially on the reason for my brother's anger and the reason for my anger. To make a long story short, she said the following words, "Seidn kukn sich, problem." ("Unless you look at yourself, there will be a bigger problem.") What she taught me was that I must take responsibility for myself, that I must look at my own behavior and determine if I am engaging in it solely to avoid a difficult and anxious situation. This is not easy to do, but the more one does it, the easier it becomes!

I finally admitted that I blamed my brother to take his focus away from me. I finally told him the truth and apologized to him. He accepted my apology better than I had anticipated—though he wasn't pleasant!

Stress and Relaxation

Stress is ubiquitous. Everybody in the twenty-first century seems to be multi-tasking. Stress comes in many different forms. We often become stressed when we have too much to do in a particular time frame. Since we must all deal with stress, the key is to learn how to handle it. One simple way to prevent overextending yourself is not to say yes when you really want to say no. Another simple way to avoid stress is to leave extra time to complete a task so that you will not feel harried.

Because life is so hectic, we all need a mental and physical "breather" in order to continue with our tempestuous lives. Relaxation is good for the soul. As a little girl, I was always amazed at how calm, serene, and at peace my grandmother seemed to be. Even though she had a disability, she merely made it incidental to the rest of her life. She spent a great deal of time sitting at our kitchen table and drinking hot tea in a glass—a glass that had originally contained a memorial candle that was lit on important Jewish holidays to honor and remember deceased loved ones.

As a little girl, my routine was to come home from school, change into play clothes, and go outside to play with my friends (times were very different then!). But before I ran outside, my grandmother insisted that I sit quietly with her and listen to her favorite music. I remember always enjoying this time of day, not because I was eating a Mallomar cookie, but because time seemed to slow down for me.

During these fifteen minutes, I enjoyed the cookie, music, and conversation about school. When my grandmother sensed that I had finished my snack, she always said, *"Opru gut, for schpas."* ("Rest is good, now have fun.") When she walked me to the door so that I could play with my friends, she always said the same bewildering words to me: *"Darfn awekleign gas maschin."* ("We always need to put gas in the car.")

As I got older I realized what she had meant by those words. We all need to take time to slow down and enjoy some quality time—with ourselves. So I began a new routine. I started to take ten minutes out of my day to spend on myself. Some days I listened to music; other days I might drive to the corner store and pick out a card that I would like to receive. I mailed that card to myself—yes, to myself. Who better to receive those words that I loved?

Each day I take a ten minute break, no matter where I am. I figure that if I had diarrhea I would have to spend that much time in the bathroom anyway … without enjoying myself!

As a grandma myself, I enjoy spending time with all of my grandchildren. Even though it is hectic, I find it relaxing because so much loved is shared. I remember a day when one of my granddaughters came home from school all stressed out. She had a project due and a test to study for. She had left one of her important books at school. She was ready to burst out crying. I put my arms around her, sat her down, and gave her a Mallomar cookie and milk. She began to relax.

After about fifteen minutes of comfort and relaxation I helped her to slow down and prioritize and to budget her time more effectively. We also drove to the school to get the book that she had forgotten. Because she was relaxed, she was able to concentrate on her school work. She came through with flying colors—and she thanked her own "Dr. Grandma." That's me!

I often pick up my grandchildren after school. Isa, Ale, and Andre live in Florida, and I enjoy helping them relax after their hard day at school. Isa has her driver's permit, so she practices driving around town. When she first started driving she said, "Grandma, what should I do? I see a car over there!" She finally understands that she, too, is one of those drivers of a car. She always enjoys her time spent with her Dr. Grandma.

Ale loves to complete a portion of her homework before we go to Nordstrom's, just the two of us. We always eat the same food, onion soup. We love eating the hot and gooey melted cheese. It's heavenly for both of us, even though we generally burn our mouths! She always looks forward to her special time with her Dr. Grandma.

Andre loves to unwind after school with a videogame, swim, or basketball game. We often compete with each other, and he generally wins, even though I really do try to win. He, too, thoroughly enjoys his quality time with his Dr. Grandma.

My grandson Jacob lives in New Jersey, so I do not see him as often as I see my grandchildren in Florida. But I still manage to spend quality time with him. I generally pick him up from his daycare center and take him to the park to see the ducks. He quacks along with them. He loves them from afar, but when they come closer, he seems to have a change of heart!

If one grandma is good, then two grandmothers must be great! Often Jacob's other grandmother, Nina, spends the day with us. We have a routine of going to Starbucks, to the park to see the ducks, and to lunch. Naptime follows for Jacob and his "two grannies!" Nina and I are often pooped but invigorated. There is nothing like the special bond between a child and his or her grandma.

I always repeat my grandmother's words when it is relaxation time: *"Darfn awekleign gas maschin."* ("We always need to put gas in the car.") Since my grandchildren do not speak Yiddish, they often create an English counterpart to my grandmother's words. In this particular case it is, "Barf away, gas station." I have often overheard my grandchildren say these words to their friends when they are stressed and apparently want to take a Mallomar time-out.

Bubbie, your words are living on—thank you!

Even today when I have a glass of hot tea and bite into the "relaxation cookie," I relish the soft chocolate and marshmallow combination. It is heavenly and so relaxing. Most important, it takes me back to my childhood with Grandma!

What Grandma said:

Take a warm bath; it's good for the soul.

Have a cup of warm milk.

Curl up with a good book.

Come, let's watch Ed Solomon on television. (She meant Ed Sullivan.)

Get some rest; you look tired.

Smell the beautiful flowers.

You won't be able to do anything right because you're doing too many things at the same time.

Look, look at that beautiful butterfly.

Come, let's look at the birds.

Listen to the rain; it sounds so good.

Moshe is sad with no play.

What Grandma said:

Take time for you; it's important.

Don't just do for the others; you've got
to take care of yourself too.

Go have fun. You'll do the rest of the homework later.

Let's do whatever makes you happy now.

Let's just do nothing and enjoy it.

Let's go to the beach and have fun. We'll
make sand castles and pick shells.

You're doing too much; you're gonna get crazy.

You're running and running yourself into the ground.

Go for a bike ride; it'll do you good.

Call a friend; you'll feel better.

Calm down; it's going to be all right.

Enough already; slow down. *Oy gevalt.*

Memory:

One day when I was about ten years old I ran into my house after school to get my bicycle so that I could ride to my friend's house. Since I knew that my grandmother liked me to have cookies and milk after school in order to relax, I guzzled my milk and crammed the whole cookie into my mouth. I sneezed, and there went the cookie all over the floor. We cleaned up the mess, and she offered me another cookie. I told her that I did not have any time. I became more and more upset that my grandmother was wasting my time. My friend was going to be waiting for me, and I did not want to be late.

To increase my stress level even more, my grandmother told me that she wanted to show me something special before I went to my play date. She took me into my back yard to do something important, she claimed. My grandmother bent down to touch the flowers. As we approached the lilac bush that was behind the flower beds she said, "Shelenkeh, kumn schmekn blum, wichtik ophaltn natur, opschazn." (Come smell the beautiful flowers; it's important to appreciate nature, to stop for nature—to relax.)

She was trying to tell me that I needed to stop doing so many activities and take time to relax, to appreciate beauty and nature. She was so happy just smelling the flowers, even though she could not see the beautiful purple color. Together, we gathered a bunch of flowers for me to bring to my friend. My friend was very excited about the flowers. She put them into a vase with water and set them in the middle of her kitchen table. The atmosphere was so serene that we decided to sit at her kitchen table, have cookies and milk, and, above all, admire the beautiful flowers.

My grandmother made me appreciate taking time out of life to enjoy the little things that don't cost money. I guess that is why I always have a vase of beautiful flowers in my home. I calm down every time I look at them and devour their scent. By the way, my children always have beautiful flowers in their homes as well. Thanks, Bubbie!

Self-Esteem

Self-esteem is not something one can buy. It is something one feels inside. We tend to view ourselves based on the way we believe others perceive us. When we feel good about ourselves, our self-esteem is positive. When we feel bad about ourselves, our self-esteem is negative. When I was young and my brother helped me with homework, he invariably ended up by calling me *stupid*. Even though my grades were excellent, I still felt stupid.

There were no compliments from my parents to counteract this negative feeling that I had about myself. I always wanted my parents to attend my parent/teacher conferences because I knew that the teachers would provide them with rave reviews about me. They said that they would attend if I were failing classes, but the fact that I was receiving all A's made it unnecessary. I would never do that to my own children!

My grandmother always told me that I was pretty, smart, and a good person. This was always followed by the following words: *"Merste wichtik men gleibn."* ("The most important thing is that you believe it yourself; nobody else can give it to you.") She always had me repeat the words, *"Shelenkeh, siskeit, klug."* ("Sheila, so sweet and smart.") In the end I started to believe those words.

When our self-esteem is negative, we tend to engage in self-defeating behaviors. The trick is to understand how to feel good about yourself. Start with a daily affirmation; say to yourself, "I am a valuable individual; I like myself."

Thank you, Bubbie.

What Grandma said:

I'm so proud of you.

You are a very important person.

All gone; what a good job!

I know you can do that; I believe in you.

I love you; now love yourself.

You are beautiful on the inside too.

You're not too short; you're perfect for Grandma.

You're not ugly; you're beautiful—go see in the mirror.

My *shayna maidel* (my pretty girl).

My *zeesee boychik* (my sweet boy).

What Grandma said:

Of course you're not too tall; you're just right!

Grandma loves you so much.

My granddaughter is brilliant, brilliant, I tell you.

My grandson, so smart—I know he'll
be a doctor some day.

I don't want to brag, but these kids are
definitely smarter than other kids.

Listen good, listen to what she said—so
smart and beyond her years.

She'll be a big success when she gets older.

Oy, he's such a smart cookie.

Oy, my *kinder* (kids) are so special.

Memory:

When I was about twelve years old, I went to get my bicycle so that I could go into town with my friends. When I went into the garage, I saw that the seat was crooked and that one screw was missing. I did, however, find the screw on the floor. I was really upset because my friends and I were going to buy a birthday present for another one of our friends. Needless to say, I was not very happy. When I explained the situation to my mother, she merely said, "You will just have to wait until your father comes home tonight." No empathy!

My grandmother overheard the conversation and told me that she thought I could fix the bicycle myself. I thought she had lost her mind! I wasn't a mechanic. She told me that I was very smart and if my father told me, over the telephone, how to do it, I would probably be able to repair the bicycle seat. Over and over, my grandmother kept saying to me, "Ich gleibn men; men gescheit, feiik." ("I believe in you; you are smart, capable.") The more she repeated the words, the more I began to believe her. She had such faith in me that I began to have faith in myself.

I called my father at work. He told me what tool to use and where to find it in the tool box. He explained in detail how to use the wrench and screw driver. I couldn't believe it. I actually fixed the seat! I hugged my grandmother and felt as though I could accomplish anything if I tried really hard and believed in myself.

To this day, whenever I think that something may be too difficult for me to accomplish, I think back to my grandmother's words. I realize that if I put my ingenuity to work I will be successful—and I usually am! If I try and try to no avail, I always ask for help, and that's okay too. Remember, we cannot be good at everything, but we must not be afraid to try something that we think might be too difficult! You never know; you might even succeed!

Change

Life is full of change, and we must learn to adapt in order to grow and thrive. Sometimes an unexpected accident, illness, or medical procedure goes awry, and our whole life is turned upside down. We have two choices. We can lament over what happened and remain inert, or we can say, "So what can I do now?" The latter gives us one problem to deal with, while the former gives us two problems to deal with (the issue itself and the inertia).

When I was a little girl I had a dog who had been hit by a car. The dog lived but had extensive injuries. She was unable to use one of her paws. It was very sad. I lamented for weeks over the unfortunate circumstance. My grandmother told me, *"Onnemn beitn abscess best."* ("Take the change; make the best.") She was telling me to accept what had happened and to adapt to the new situation. After some time, I began to listen to her words.

I played games with the dog that did not involve running. Over time, the dog also adapted to the change and began to run as quickly as she had before the accident. I realized that by accepting the change and adapting to it, life returned to a new kind of normal.

Another area of change involves relationships. As a child I always felt anxious whenever my brother came home from school. My mother frequently told him to help me with my homework. The same outcome repeated itself. My brother would say to me, "You're stupid—why can't you get it?" I wondered why he couldn't understand that calling me cruel names was hurtful and insensitive. After being chided for it, he stopped calling me *stupid*, but his body language indicated that he found me to be of somewhat lower intelligence.

After a session with my brother, my grandmother usually came to sit with me at my desk. She would invariably say to me, *"Nor men iberbetn, men nit iberbetn an ande."* ("We can change ourselves but not others.") I really had no idea what she was talking about.

She helped me to explore other options regarding getting help in math. I realized that if I stayed late after school, one of my friends would help me with my homework. My mother agreed to pick me up from school at a later time. That seemed to solve the problem.

I realized that my grandmother was telling me that I could not change my brother, no matter how hard I tried. I also understood that by changing my reaction to my brother, I could initiate a change myself. I stopped taking help from him and instead was helped by my friend, who was patient and understanding. Because I felt comfortable asking her questions, I improved my math skills. After a short period of time I no longer needed math help.

To this day, I realize that I cannot change another person; I can only change myself; above all, *I can change my response to others.*

By the way, once my brother was no longer my math tutor, our relationship changed for the better! We always look forward to seeing each other today.

What Grandma said:

The only one you can change is
yourself—you better believe it!

You never know what tomorrow will bring.

Any minute, things could change.

Drive carefully. I don't want to be called
that you were in an accident.

We don't ask for sickness, it just comes.

Things change … some for the
better, some for the worse.

You can't change him; try changing yourself.

That's not working; try something else!

Memory:

When I was about nine years old I had to do a project for my history class. I decided to use the inside of a shoe box to depict the story of George Washington crossing the Delaware River. I misjudged the space size and kept trying to place artifacts that were too large into the box. No matter how I tried to place the pieces, they did not fit. Naturally, I became frustrated, and I started to throw the items on the floor.

My grandmother overheard the commotion and sat down beside me. She asked me what I was upset about. I explained the situation. She placed her hands inside the shoe box and touched all of the items that I wanted to include in my project. She finally said to me, "Kein mol nit ganzn in ganzn; pruwn andersch." ("Never will they all fit; try something different.") It was then that I realized that she was correct in her assessment. I hadn't realized the futility of what I was attempting.

My grandmother did not do the project herself because that was my responsibility, but she did help me to brainstorm potential changes. I finally decided that I would combine drawings with two of the original artifacts. Once I made the decision to make the change, the project went quickly and smoothly. While she did teach me to persevere in the face of adversity, she also taught me to be realistic. Now, whenever I recognize that something that I am doing is futile, I immediately make a change. I also taught my children that beyond a certain point repetition is futile and unproductive, and they agree!

Loss and Grief

We all deal with various types of loss throughout our lives. Those are the times that we need a supportive and nurturing environment. While life is a journey that ought to be lived to its fullest, death is the destination for all. I remember when my grandmother passed away. It was the saddest day of my life. She was at home, surrounded by family. My cousin and I were holding her hands. We were both crying.

The doctor had come to our home and told us that it was a matter of time. We were all devastated. My grandmother was the person who actually held the family together. She told us, *"Seson beitn gornit oif eibik lebn zapl sof."* ("Seasons come and go; nothing is forever. Life has a start and a finish.") She wanted us to know that she was ready for her ending because her long life had been good to her.

She hoped that her family would act as a conduit to keep her legacy alive. Her goal was to have her cohesive family support each other during her absence. She wanted us to accept death as a natural part on the continuum of life. She helped us to believe that grief was natural but that we should not grieve forever. She told us that she wanted us to move forward in our lives and make her proud. With her last breath she said to all of us, *"Ich arbetn oibn, dich arbetn untn."* ("I will work from above, and you will work from below.") I guess she was telling us that she would be our guardian angel.

The feelings of loss and grief are not associated with death alone. Loss of job, home, health, marriage, income, and friendship may elicit the same feelings. And so, irrespective of the loss, my grandmother's teachings apply. When I lost my good health as a young adult, I recalled my grandmother's philosophy and utilized her wisdom. I decided to be grateful for what I could do and not focus on what I could not do. I did grieve my loss but not over a lifetime. At one point, I realized that I had to adapt to my new reality. I ended up by helping other handicapped mothers who were also saddened by their losses.

We must take responsibility and forge ahead in the face of loss, even if it is painful. For, in the end, the actions of life involve the living. Whenever I want to access my grandmother, I look over my right shoulder and see her in my mind's eye. I feel her warmth, tenderness, and love. I convert her loss into a gain, because she will always be in my heart, ready to help me in any situation.

What Grandma said:

May he rest in peace.

We're all here for you.

Come, sit on Grandma's lap.

Look, all your friends came; they liked grandpa.

Time is a wonderful healer.

Thank G-d he/she is out of his/her misery.

We all have to die some day.

We will remember her always, with love.

She's looking out for us as your guardian angel now.

What Grandma said:

Always think about the good times together.

Oh, how he loved you!

He would want you to stop crying.

I'll sit next you; I won't talk, but I'm
right here if you need me.

Crying is good.

At least she is at peace; no more suffering.

The end, we were all there; we made good.

Memory:

When I was a little girl my father bought me an adorable hamster that I named Hymie. He was my pride and joy and I diligently took care of him. One morning, before leaving for school, I went to feed Hymie. I thought it was rather strange that I did not hear any of his normal squealing sounds. When I looked in his cage he was crouched in a corner. He was still alive, but he did not seem like his normal self. I was very worried.

My mother promised that while I was in school, she would take Hymie to the pet store where we purchased him. The first thing I did when I came home from school was to look in Hymie's cage. He was still there, but he looked even worse than he had in the morning. My mother told me that Hymie was very ill and that there was no medicine that would help him. I started to cry uncontrollably.

My grandmother knew how upset I was, and she sat with me and watched Hymie. She suggested that we make Hymie comfortable by leaving fresh water and food for him in case he wanted some. She also said that we should put on some music to sooth Hymie. My grandmother told me, "Lebn kein mol nit schtendik toit natirlech end reise." ("Life is never permanent; death is the end of the journey.") She stayed with me until Hymie passed away and said, "Passik umetik nischt derschrokn, gedenkn." ("It's okay to be sad but not afraid; remember.")

She was trying to tell me that we are all on a temporary journey on earth; birth is at the beginning and death is at the end. I learned that I must accept death as a natural and normal event that happens to all living creatures. She wanted me to remember that the final journey should include comfort and compassion, but not fear.

I realize now that providing water and food for Hymie kept me occupied and allowed me to take some kind of action on Hymie's *behalf. The music calmed both of us. When my own uncle was on his end-of-life journey, my family and I surrounded him. Music played; there was water on the table and a bowl full of delicious smelling lavender. We made sure that Uncle Jack was safe and comfortable on his final journey. My family and I grieve when a death occurs, but we do not fear. Thank you, Bubbie, for teaching me that all who have passed away still remain in our loving hearts ... especially you!*

Enjoy Life ... Happy Thoughts ... Status

The Buddhists believe that we are our own thoughts. According to Buddha, "We are what we think. All that we are arises with our thoughts. With our thoughts we make our world." We have the choice to frame our thoughts any way that we wish. By framing our thoughts in a positive, rather than negative, manner, we are better able to think happy thoughts. Happy thoughts can help to brighten our day and relieve some of our stresses. Too often we focus on material possessions and say to ourselves, "If only I had this, if only I had that ..." But with each new acquisition we tend to want more. So when is enough, enough?

Will we ever be able to catch up? Will we always look to the future and forget the present? Why are so many of us caught up in the whirlwind of competing with others for status symbols? We tend to look at what others have and judge them based on their material possessions. According to the Dalai Lama, "The secret of happiness lies in the mind's release from worldly ties." It is important to like people for who they are rather than what they have.

While some may have more than we do, others have less. We must not think less of those who do not have as much as we do. It is important to be grateful for what we do have and not lament over what we do not have. It is not the amount of dollars and cents that makes an individual who he or she is; it is the amount of sense he or she possesses and utilizes on a daily basis.

When I was about thirteen years old I became friends with a new girl at school. Her family was very wealthy, and she had all of the material possessions that anyone could hope for. My attitude about life began to change after we met. I began to want the same kind of expensive clothing that she had. When I asked to buy some of the things that she had, my mother told me that we could not afford to buy them. She invariably said, "Be grateful; some other kids don't even have what you have."

After discussions such as these, I invariably locked myself in my room and felt very sad. I often remained morose because I felt cheated. One day my grandmother asked me to come out of my room and sit with her while she had a glass of tea. I knew that some kind of lesson was about to ensue. She told me about how difficult her life was in the Old Country and how hard she had to work. She had to help her mother with household chores even before going to school. Even though her life seemed difficult, not one that I would have liked to emulate, she did not seem angry or resentful.

She explained that her father was a tailor and that her mother cleaned other people's houses. She always wore hand-me-down clothing that her mother received from friends whose children had outgrown them. When I asked her why she wasn't angry, she said, *"Ich arbetn neitik dankbar; ich mer ander; far wos troierik narisch."* -- ("I worked hard, it was necessary; I had more than others; foolish to be angry.")

When I listened to her words, I realized that I was being very selfish. I had not given thanks for all of the wonderful people and things I had in my life. I began to count my blessings. I moved away from negativity and made wiser, more positive choices.

I began to think about a girl in my class who had just lost her father. Apparently, money was an issue for the family, because the girl wore shoes that had holes in the soles. I went to my piggy bank and told my grandmother that I wanted to spend my money on a pair of shoes for that girl. My grandmother was so happy that she said, *"Wi mecheie mensch."* ("How wonderful! You are such a good person—be happy.") To this day I make sure that I give unused clothing to a variety of charities, and that always puts a smile on my face! Thank you, Bubbie, for helping me with my priorities!

What Grandma said:

Think about today—not yesterday,
not tomorrow ; enjoy now.

Don't think other people always have it better than you.

Enjoy every minute of every day.

Boy, is that sky blue; look—it's a rainbow!

Just have fun; it's good for you.

Go to a dance; who knows, you
might find somebody you like.

Let's go to the beach, look at the
ocean, and collect shells.

A smile is good, a happy face too.

Money isn't everything. Don't try to keep
up with others who have more.

There's always someone worse off.

What Grandma said:

The reward for a life that is good is that good life.

You can meet the same people
going up as coming down.

Don't get too big for your pants.

It doesn't have to be expensive to be nice.

Don't take anything for granted.

Don't let all that money go to your head.

Don't try to be a big shot; humble is better.

Boy, nobody can stand a show-off!

Don't think you're better than everybody
else just because you have money.

Don't look down on others just because
they don't have what you have.

Memory:

One afternoon a group of my friends came to my house after school. We listened to music and began to gossip about the other students in our class. We invariably talked about all of the boys that we liked. We crooned over the good-looking boys who paid no attention to us. At one point in the conversation, my friends began to talk about one of the boys who was good-looking and smart but poorly dressed.

He did not wear fashionable clothing; most of what he wore did not fit him properly. Some items were much too tight, while others were too loose and baggy. We knew that his sister's clothing was also in poor condition. In fact, the mother of these two students worked as a domestic for the parents of some of my friends. I knew that it was not very nice to speak in this vein about people who had less than we all had. But I did not have the guts to speak up.

Apparently my grandmother heard us. She invited all of us to have cookies and milk with her while she drank her tea. Since my friends loved my grandmother, they were eager to sit with her and have a snack. I, on the other hand, was very nervous, because I knew that my grandmother probably did not appreciate my silence on the subject. My grandmother told us stories, in her broken English, about how she looked like a ragamuffin as a child because her family was poor. She also told us about a situation in which one of her friends at school had made fun of her. My Bubbie had tears in her eyes when she told us the story.

My friends and I all looked at each other with sadness. We immediately knew that what we were doing was very wrong. Then my grandmother said to us, "Denkn, fartreter person?" ("Think—do you want to substitute for that person?") She was trying to help us to be compassionate and empathetic instead of catty. She showed us firsthand how hurtful and disrespectful we were to think less of somebody because he or she did not have what we had. From that day on, we always invited those students to our birthday parties. They were so happy, but because of what my Bubbie had taught us, we were even happier!

Health, Personal Hygiene, and Moderation

My grandmother was a very simple and practical person who tried to live a healthy lifestyle. She tried to do everything in moderation so that she could remain balanced, which she was. She knew the value of good nutrition, preventative medicine, and regular exercise. Her intuition was incredible. She sensed that mind and body needed to be in sync.

My grandmother taught us lessons about this subject on weekends, when there was no school. The teachings began at our Shabbat dinners (Friday night dinners before the Sabbath). My grandmother always talked about the food that was on our plates and how it contributed to our health. Though she never used the words such as *protein, dairy, carbohydrates,* and *starches,* she always encouraged us to drink milk so that we would have strong bones and to eat fruits and vegetables so that we would have vitamins, minerals, and nutrients. Her words were always the same: *"Schpeis energie."* ("Food gives you energy.")

Because Shabbat (Saturday) was a day of rest, we spent the day at the synagogue. My brother and I were not excited to spend the day there, needless to say. But my grandmother often said the following words to us: *"Moiech oprn noch jedie."* ("Minds needs rest to put in more information.") Since driving in a car was forbidden on the day of rest, we walked great distances to the synagogue and then to return home. When we complained that we were tired, she always said, *"Guf schtark."* ("Bodies need to be active to remain strong.")

My Bubbie provided us with a foundation for healthy living. In addition, she was very careful to let us know that we needed to work hard, to play hard, and to rest hard. She did not want us to overdo; she wanted us to understand that too much or too little of a good thing was not a good thing. Personal hygiene was important to her, as well. She encouraged us to take daily baths and wear clean clothing. She seemed ahead of her time because she focused on how crucial it was to have mind and body in a balanced position.

What Grandma said:

I think maybe if you eat fruit every
day you won't get sick.

Take an umbrella so you won't get all wet and chilled.

Bananas and spinach are good for
you; they help you grow.

Don't drink from his glass; he has a cold.

You need a good night's sleep.

Cover your mouth when you cough;
I don't want to get sick.

Don't swim right after you eat; you'll get a cramp.

Just take the medicine; it will make you feel all better.

Come, let's go for a walk; it's good exercise.

Let's go to bed; you need to get up early for school.

Let's use a fine comb on your hair, just in case.

Have a glass of milk with your cookie;
milk is good for your bones.

What Grandma said:

Don't overeat; you could throw up.

Take your vitamins; they help you grow.

Wear a hat in the sun; take lotion so you won't burn.

Don't let a dog lick your face; he licks his own *tooshie*.

Brush your teeth before you go to bed;
don't use your brother's toothbrush.

You need a shower, but don't pee in there.

Wash your hands after you go to the
bathroom; no spreading germs.

It's important to be neat and clean.

Don't drink from someone else's glass.

Don't burn the candle at both ends.

Slow down, you could choke.

You cannot take the head away from the body.

Memory:

After I had chicken pox as a child, I was very tired. All I wanted to do was to stay in bed and watch television. At one point, the doctor told my mother that I was improving but I needed to engage in more activity. My mother asked me if I wanted to get out of bed, and I said no. She did not encourage me any further and left my bedroom.

On the other hand, my grandmother came into my bedroom and sat on my bed. Her mere presence gave me inspiration. She said to me, "Bleibn hoile gesunt." ("Stay a sick person or get healthy.") She was letting me know that I had a choice: to remain in bed and stay sick or to take responsibility for myself and take action to become healthy. She extended her hand to me and said, "Genitunk gut, kumn." ("Exercise is good; come.") There was no hesitation on my part. I stood up, got dressed, gave my Bubbie a hug, and went for a walk with her. It was heavenly walking along with her and holding hands. Even as I talk about this, I feel her soft fingers clasping mine. It was so heavenly!

Manners

Manners are standards of conduct that are unenforceable. They indicate whether an individual is acting properly: polite and refined. Manners are like laws because they set a standard for human behavior, but they are unlike laws in that there is no formal system for punishment, other than social disapproval. They are a kind of norm. My grandmother was a stickler for table manners. She was very particular about not placing elbows on the table, especially if someone sat next to her, because she could not see what was going on around her. She often told us, *"Nischt elnboygn tish schlekht."* ("No elbows on the table; it shows bad upbringing.")

Sometimes I was allowed to have a friend share Shabbat dinner with us. I remember a situation in which a rather chubby friend of mine was sitting at our Shabbat table. She sat in between my grandmother and me. In between the matzo ball soup and the chopped liver, my mother went around the table collecting the soup bowls. My friend placed her elbows on the table and tipped over some of her remaining soup. It fell into my grandmother's lap and seeped through her napkin and onto her Shabbat dress. She was a lady and said to my friend, *"Tsufal firkumen; nischt gedeyget."* ("An accident; don't worry about it.") After my parents left to drive my friend home, my grandmother said to me and my brother, *"Zen, Nisht geshent mit klal."* ("You better realize this; without good manners and rules this can happen.")

Good manners were of paramount importance to my grandmother. They were synonymous with good breeding and upbringing. She encouraged me to be considerate of other people, to engage in tact and diplomacy, and to be hospitable to guests. Today I practice hospitality and good manners, and all of my friends tell me that I am a delightful hostess.

Having good manners is very important even today, as evidenced by the copious amount of books, advice columns, and schools that deal with this subject. Each of us has the choice to become a lady or a gentleman. I guess I equate good manners with being considerate of others. I taught my grandmother's philosophy to my children. Whenever they had a play date, invariably the friend's mother would say to me, "Your children are so well behaved, and they always say *please* and *thank you*."

What Grandma said:

Use your napkin; put it in your lap.

Cover your mouth and nose when
you sneeze; I'll get a tissue.

Don't pick your nose; use a tissue.

Don't forget to say *please* and *thank you*.

Be considerate to everybody, not just old people.

Don't jump on the sofa.

I'm busy; have patience.

Consideration, respect for others—this is important.

Don't eat with your fingers; use the silverware.

What Grandma said:

Take your hat off in the house; be a gentleman.

Don't cough in someone's face.

Offer your seat to an old lady when you go on the trolley car.

A lady always crosses her legs.

Keep it to yourself; don't gossip.

Always carry a handkerchief in your bag; you never know when you might need it.

Memory:

My mother was an excellent cook. Friday night dinner was an important ritual for her, and the menu was always the same: chopped liver, chicken soup, chicken, candied sweet potatoes, and homemade applesauce. Before going outside to play with my friends I always stuck my fingers into the sweet potato bowl and took out a piece of sweet potato. It had a gooey sauce that often fell on the floor and became sticky. My grandmother would always say to me, "Nischt balekn zikh, banitsn gopl-lefl farhitn." ("Don't use your fingers. Use silverware, and that won't happen.")

I could not figure out how my grandmother knew what I was doing. When I asked her, she told me that she heard me slurping and then turning on the water at the sink to wet a sponge so that I could clean up the mess before my mother saw it. I must admit that, even today, when I make my mother's sweet potato recipe, I pick up a piece with my fingers! But not out in public; my grandmother would be outraged.

Diversity and Discrimination

We live in a pluralistic society, with many diverse groups of individuals. Identity is at our core. We often view ourselves from the reactions that we receive from others and act upon that basis. When I worked as a social worker in the drug and alcohol rehab, I saw many patients who had been told at very young ages that they were *losers*. These individuals not only believed that they were, in fact, losers, but they engaged in behaviors that confirmed and reinforced the label … to their detriment.

My grandmother often told me, *"Redn negative oysdn ikn zikh meynen; nischt."* ("If you think badly about yourself you will believe it; don't do that.") I often tell my patients an abbreviated version of my grandmother's words: "Say bad things about yourself, and you believe them." Those words always help my patients to gain a great deal of insight into the negative labels that they carry within them.

Ultimately, they understand that those who had given them the derogatory labels were the perpetrators and that they were actually the victims. In the end the victims converted their labels from *victim* to *survivor*. Only then were they able to move forward in a positive direction. My grandmother understood this concept well, even though she had no formal training.

In my own life, I grew up with little self-esteem. My brother often called me derogatory names about my intelligence level, and my mother did not intervene and punish him for his cruel words. I believed in the label I had been given. And so in my younger days, I always defended myself when it was not even necessary.

I believe that my original educational plan to receive my PhD stemmed from the fact that I was going to prove to everybody that I was, in fact, smart. As I grew older I realized that the *stupid* label had followed me, but only because I allowed it to. I realized that I was the only one who could convert my label of *stupid* to *smart*. And so I did. Boy, was that liberating! I also realized that while individuals were often given negative labels, some groups also were given negative labels. But not in my house!

As a child, I lived in a very diverse neighborhood: race, color, ethnicity, religion, gender, and age. My family always went to the homes of Christian neighbors at holiday time to decorate a Christmas tree or to participate in an Easter egg hunt. Likewise, neighbors came to our Jewish home on holidays to participate in the religious ceremonies and to eat matzo balls, gefilte fish, and chopped liver. Always after a celebration with neighbors, my grandmother would say, *"Andersch ober selbik, ale gut."* ("Different but same; all good.")

She taught me to value and respect all human beings. She stressed that even though each of us is unique, we share more commonalities than differences. I am proud to say that my family is quite diverse. My dad used to say that our family was just like the United Nations!

What Grandma said:

We are all equal—maybe different, but equal.

Don't ever be mean to anybody who is old
or sick or has a different skin color.

Don't be so quick to judge.

Live and let live.

It's good to know the neighbors; they are good people.

You won't like everyone, and not everyone will like you.

We are all different on the outside
but the same on the inside.

What Grandma said:

Not everybody takes things the same way.

Some people are handicapped and in wheelchairs; don't stare; inside is the same.

Some people are old and some are young; respect all of them.

We are so lucky that there are so many different kinds of people.

It's so good to know lots of different kinds of people.

The inside is what counts.

We all need to use toilet paper—remember that!

Memory:

I used to ride my bicycle with my friends after school. One day a friend of mine decided to invite her cousin over to visit. She did not have her own bicycle, so we each took turns lending her ours. Whenever it was time for her to give us back our bicycles, she laughed and rode around the block. She did this numerous times. When I finally went into the house, I was very frustrated. I told my mother what had happened, and she told me not to worry about it. On the other hand, my grandmother overheard the conversation and heard me say that I hated the girl.

My grandmother told me, "In di welt nit jeder eine gefeln fein." ("In this world not everybody likes everybody, and that is okay.") She was telling me that I did not have to hate anybody and give them a negative label because they had different values than I did. She finally told me that it was important to be respectful but to understand that I would not like everybody I encountered in life. She also told me that it was equally important for me to remember that not everyone would like me either. That was bitter sweet. But I did remember the words of my grandmother during a conversation I had later in life with one of my sisters-in-law.

One day my sister-in-law called and asked me, for the sake of being married to brothers, if we could be cordial to each other. She told me that she did not like me and knew that I did not like her. I was taken aback, because although I knew that I did not particularly care for her, I wondered why she did not like me. I guess what my Bubbie said was true. At any rate, I respected her honesty, and we have a good relationship today.

Being Gullible

We have to become critical thinkers in order to understand the reality of the world around us. We cannot believe everything that people say to us. Some individuals are unsavory and may try to fool us into believing something that is not true. When I was a little girl I loved to watch the *I Love Lucy Show*. My grandmother loved to listen to the clever comedy. She even sat right in front of the television. I guess she could see shadows; at the very least, she heard all of the dialogue.

In one episode, Lucy, Ricky, Ethel, and Fred were in Paris. Each went off on his or her own and bought a painting from what they each believed was a starving artist who would one day become famous. The artist was very convincing, telling them that the painting would be worth a great deal of money in the future. Upon returning to the hotel they decided to share their good fortune with each other. To each one's horror, they all had the same picture, which had probably been a paint-by-number canvas. They were all horrified that they had been duped by the fast-talking conniver.

My grandmother asked me if I knew what had happened in the scenario. I wasn't exactly sure. She told me, *"Sein forsihtik nit nar ligner."* ("Be careful. Don't be a fool; crooks out there.") What she was really trying to tell me was to be cautious and to beware of unscrupulous con artists. I guess she understood the meaning of the words, "Let the buyer beware!" I always try to look at what is rather than what I would like it to be. It usually works, but sometimes even I can be fooled! Life is not an exact science, I guess. Try to be realistic, and use reason over emotion. By the way, I still watch the *I Love Lucy* reruns. Even though I can recite each of the character's lines, I still laugh out loud! Watching *I Love Lucy*, for me, is better than taking a Valium!

What Grandma said:

Don't believe everything you hear.

Don't be foolish; money is hard to make.

You better not try to fool me; it won't work.

Don't listen to him; he doesn't know
what he's talking about.

I thought you were smarter than that.

You paid *what* for that piece of garbage
that's not worth anything?

If it's big, don't believe it's better; maybe
sometimes yes, maybe sometimes no.

You get what you pay for.

If you think it's too good to be true,
you're probably right.

What Grandma said:

He sure fooled you; you don't get
something for nothing.

A bargain is not always a bargain; that's junk.

If you believe that, I've got some land
in to sell you in a swamp.

You're on your own with this one.

How crazy is that!

Don't just look at the frosting on the cake.
Maybe the inside doesn't taste so good.

Don't look at the world through glasses that are pink.

Don't get suckered in!

Memory:

I was invited to a birthday party for one of my friends who had a large, beautiful home. I knew that her family was wealthy because my friend always wore cashmere sweaters and shiny loafers with pennies in them. All of the girls were envious of her, even me. When it came time for the goody bags to be handed out, my friend said that she was not giving us a bag filled with candy and trinkets. She explained that she was giving each of us a diamond ring. We all shrieked with joy. We could not believe our good fortune. Each of us gingerly placed the rings on our fingers. It was very cold out and we decided to forgo the gloves we had worn because they would hide our sparkly diamond rings that we wanted everyone to admire.

When I got home, I was very excited. I showed the ring to my mother, who merely said, "Very nice!" I danced euphorically around the house with my glass ring on my finger. My grandmother came over to me after I stopped dancing, and she asked if she could see the ring. "Can I feel it?" I quickly placed my hand into hers and watched while she fingered the circle of the ring and then the stone. I screeched, "I can't believe it, a diamond ring! It is worth a fortune—unbelievable!" My grandmother said, "Du bist oder nischt bist, fool!" ("You are or you aren't a fool!") She was trying to tell me that because it was so "unbelievable," I better stop and think about it. She asked me if it made sense to me that my friend would really give away thirteen diamond rings to her friends. After I thought about it, it didn't make too much sense to me.

It did seem rather far-fetched. My grandmother was trying to tell me that if something seemed unrealistic, maybe it wasn't real at all. She told me that if it were a real diamond, it would scratch a glass table surface. So we went into my bedroom and used the stone to scratch the glass top on my school desk. Nothing happened. I then had proof that the ring was not a diamond but instead glass. I couldn't believe that my friend would lie and try to fool us. My grandmother taught me that anybody, even a good friend, might try to fool me, but that I could be fooled only if I allowed it. Today, I always take a second look at something that seems unbelievable! Beware; there are lots of scam artists out there.

Communication and Effective Listening

Communication is an interaction between at least two people. It's a system for sending and receiving messages and involves the sharing of ideas and information. There is a sender and a receiver. Since our reactions to situations tend to be both subjective and reflexive, the receiver of the message may misinterpret the intentions of the sender.

One day my husband told me that he had changed plane reservations that we had made together. Immediately, I began to think that he wanted to control the situation and prevent me from being part of the new decision. My grandmother always said, *"Nit paskenen; fregn erscht, hern gut, told."* ("Don't judge so fast; ask first, and listen good.") She was trying to tell me that I was not a mind reader, nor did I know anyone's intentions. Her recommendation was to ask questions and clarify what someone was telling me before becoming angry and jumping to conclusions.

So instead of reacting emotionally, I responded rationally. I asked my husband what his intentions had been in changing a joint decision without informing me. I was shocked at his answer: "I know that you don't like to take very early flights, and I found reservations for later in the day. I knew that would make you happy." I had been tempted to respond according to what had happened previously in our marriage. But in this situation I had decided to follow my grandmother's advice—which seems to work all the time! I had not overreacted and caused my husband to become defensive.

Communication may be oral or written, but it may also be nonverbal. The body language of an individual can also communicate a message very clearly, sometimes more so than the written or the spoken word. An additional, important component of communication is being able to listen attentively.

It is not beneficial to only listen to oneself. One must also listen carefully to others to allow for clarification in order to better understand the message of the sender. It is very important to listen to others so they will want to listen to you as well. I have been ill for so many years, and yet many of my friends still send me beautiful bouquets of flowers whenever I have a hospital stay, which unfortunately is quite often. When I ask them why they continue to be there for me each and every time, they invariably say the following, "You are such a good friend and the best listener in the world!" Remember, it doesn't cost any money to be a good listener, so give it a try.

What Grandma said:

Speak clearly; I don't understand what you're saying.

Don't mumble.

Speak up; I can't hear you.

I don't know what you are thinking in
your head, so you better tell me.

Boy, do you sound mad!

Look at that face!

That's a mean and nasty thing to say!

Don't push him; don't hit him either!

How am I supposed to know what you're thinking?

Speak like a human being. Don't yell!

What Grandma said:

What!? I'm not a mind reader.

Don't take anything for granted; speak up.

So, tell me what's bothering you, my little one.

I'll be an old lady by the time you tell me what's wrong.

Stop crying; get to the point and speak.

I heard you.

Can you explain better; I don't understand that.

Listen to your mother; she knows a lot.

You don't know everything; better
start listening to other people.

The world just doesn't work around you only.

Memory:

One day at school I found out that a friend of mine was having a birthday party to which I was invited. I was very excited about that because there was going to be a clown to entertain us. The next day at school, some of my girlfriends were whispering about the party, but when I asked them what they were talking about, they said, "Nothing special." I became aware that the birthday girl was allowed to have three friends sleep over at her house, and I was not one of the selected few. I was really upset.

When I came home from school, my mother asked me what was wrong. She could tell by the expression on my face that I was unhappy. Instead of telling her why I was upset, I started slamming doors, and I locked myself in my bedroom. My mother decided to pay no attention to me, but my grandmother did. She knocked on the door and told me to come and have cookies and milk with her while she had some tea.

I knew that there was something she wanted to talk to me about. After about ten minutes of wallowing in self-pity, I decided to join her at the kitchen table. She tried to talk to me, but I answered in monosyllables. She could tell by the sound of my voice that I was distraught. I knew that she would help me, but I decided to basically remain mute. She finally said to me in a rather stern voice, "Wer kenen wisn on redn!" ("Who can help without knowing the problem; talk already!") I loved her so much, and I always felt better after talking to her.

And so when she said those words, I realized that if I kept the situation to myself I would remain unhappy and that nobody would be able to help me because they were not mind readers. When I finally told her the problem, she helped me to understand that not everybody could be included in everything. She helped me to understand that I was invited to the party itself, where there was no limit. She indicated that I was excluded only because there was a limit for the sleepover. She stressed that I should not expect to be included in everything that others were. She also told me that I would not be included by everyone all of the time. I guess she taught me not to take things so personally.

Even today, when friends or neighbors have guests at their homes and I am not invited, I do not take it personally. I do not count cars in driveways or write down license plates, which many of my friends do! Thanks, Grandma!

Let's Have Fun, Just You and Grandma

My grandmother was a great believer in working hard, but she also encouraged me to have fun. She believed that a life without fun would be too oppressive. On a Saturday she would usually say to me, *"Haltn machn izt seier gut."* ("Stop. Now fun—it's very good for you.") Sometimes we would sing Yiddish songs that she taught me. I particularly like the one called "Der Winter, Der Merder" ("The Winter, the Assassin.") The song extolled the virtues and challenges of the snow and the wind. The tune was very soothing.

About ten years ago my husband and I took a trip to Poland. On the bus ride to each important site, our guide sang songs from the Old Country. I knew that my grandmother had lived in Poland, so I asked her if she had ever heard of the song that my grandmother used to sing to me. She said that she knew all of the words because it had been a very famous song.

And so the guide and I sang the song together. One lone tear trickled down my cheek. As I looked around at the other passengers on the bus, I noticed that they were crying too. I had chills up and down my spine as we sang the beautiful words and melody. I recorded the song on a CD, and I play it often. It always makes me happy, though I still cry.

What Grandma said:

Just for today, you can be anyone you want;
pick a name, and I'll call you that all day.

Wanna bake cupcakes? You can be the helper.

Let's play school; you can be the teacher.

At the beach we can build a sand castle.

Wanna put on grandpa's shoes and jackets?

Let's look in my closet and play dress-up.

Let's jump rope and skip down the street.

Let's sit on the stoop and draw a picture.

What Grandma said:

Today, we're going to see the animals at the zoo.

Let's get under the covers and get *snuggly, buggly*.

Let's go for a ride and get an ice cream.

Let me tell you a story, and then
you can read me a story.

Let's sing a song first. Come, I'll tuck you in.

Good night, sleep tight, and don't let the bedbugs bite.

Memory:

As a child, one of days that was the most fun for me was when I could play-act and be anyone that I wanted to be. It was like being an actress and playing a role. My grandmother always told me stories about her dog, Chonchik, whom she had to give to a friend when she came to the United States. The dog was apparently very high-spirited, energetic, and curious. She often told me how he climbed upon a table and ate a whole cake that she had made for company! How did she measure the ingredients? When I asked her she said, "Ich wisn sich a bisl dos dem, gisn arein." ("I know myself: a little this, a little that; pour it in.") Her cakes were always delicious. I cannot make her cakes today because I have no idea what "a little of this and a little of that" means.

One day I decided to be her dog, and she called my by his name all day. Every so often I would kneel at her feet and bark and bark. She patted my head and told me that I was a wonderful friend to her and that she loved me so much. Even playing the role of her dog, I knew that Chonchik must have felt her love for him. That day was one I will never forget. She taught me how to be creative with myself and not just with others. So when I wish that someone would send me flowers, I call the florist and have roses sent. When the florist asks me what I would like to say on the card, I usually respond by saying, "Chonchik, I love you and your master!" I often send myself cards with sentiments that I would like to receive. Those cards I address to myself, and I write,

"Dear Dr. Sheila ... thinking of you."

These cards are a reminder that I am a very important person!

Taking Responsibility

We cannot expect to go through life having others take on our responsibilities. We must be dependable, reliable, and dutiful. When one does not accept responsibility for oneself, one's life becomes a difficult journey. When I first became ill as a young mother, I was angry. I felt isolated and very lonely. I dreaded being home every day without anybody to speak to; it seemed unbearable.

Not only did I have a debilitating illness that prevented me from going out, but I was also becoming more unhappy by the day. Sitting in my kitchen, looking out at the beautiful crisp, white snow, I began to ask myself what my grandmother would have recommended. She always taught me that I was like a car. If I went to the end of a street that did not take me to where I wanted to go, I should turn around and look for other streets that would take me to my destination.

I realized that I was wallowing in self-pity and that I was stuck in the problem itself. In order to become part of the solution, I needed to take responsibility for myself. That meant taking some sort of action that would solve my problem. And so I did! I started a telephone support group for handicapped mothers, Comfort Call of Greater New Jersey, the first of its kind.

Even though I was housebound, I created a venue to help myself, and others as well. We were not a support group for wallowing in self pity. Rather, each of us accepted responsibility to be a crucial link in an infinite chain of strength. I had listened to my grandmother's wisdom and reached out to others in the same situation. It became a win-win for all concerned! Many newspapers wrote stories about me. My children's teachers often asked my children if I was "that lady" in the newspaper. Boy, did I feel good about myself. Bubbie, you would have been so proud of me!

What Grandma said:

The party's over.

No more free rides.

It's up to you now.

You want to get better, don't you? Then you have to take the medicine!

Take good care of yourself.

Your turn to take over now.

I'm proud of you, you're so responsible.

Look, look how he takes care of the dog!

What Grandma said:

He never forgets to take his vitamins.

She always does her homework; she's
such a good kid, so responsible.

Save for a rainy day.

Don't do anything you wouldn't want to tell me about.

Be careful when you ride your
bike; stay on the sidewalk.

You better start standing on your own two feet.

Memory:

When I was in elementary school I had many problems doing my math homework. Every day I would try to do the problems by myself, and I'd find it difficult. I did not want my older brother to help me because he always yelled at me, and I was afraid of him. He would explain how to do the problem; when he asked me to do it on my own, my fear of him was so great that I was unable to even follow his directions. Every time this happened, he ended up calling me stupid, and I ended up crying.

One of my close friends was very proficient in math, so I began calling her every day. She would walk me through the problems and provide me with all the correct answers. I was thrilled. However, when we had a test and I had to do the work on my own, I did not do well on the exam. Of course, I came home and cried. My grandmother said the following words to me: "Haltn sezn sich oifchtein zweius." ("Stop sitting down! Get up and find your own two feet.")

What she was trying to tell me was that I had to stop depending on others and start depending more on myself. She encouraged me to take my time with each problem. If I did not get the correct answer at first, she told me to do it again. After a while, I started to understand how to do the problems, because I began to stand on my own two feet, have faith in myself, and persevere, even in the face of adversity.

While I realize that it is perfectly acceptable to receive help from others, it is not beneficial to totally depend on them. It is important to believe in yourself and accept responsibility. Thanks, Grandma!

Procrastination

Many of us procrastinate, which is the habit of delaying important actions. When I was in school as an adult, I established a plan to take certain courses first because they were prerequisites to other classes. Because I had the plan in place, I guess I became rather complacent about being so organized. I waited until the last minute to sign up for one of the prerequisite classes. As a result, the class was full. Because I rationalized and justified the delay, telling myself I was too busy, I was delayed two semesters because the final class was presented once per year.

Remember, when we procrastinate we take no action. Under certain circumstances, procrastination may cause the very thing that we wanted to prevent to happen. This was my case. I guess I tested my grandmother's wisdom: *"Farhaltn tsorres."* ("Delay can cause big trouble.") I made a huge mistake by ignoring her advice.

But I am, after all, only human, and I make mistakes and errors in judgment—and that is ok. In a perfect world everything would go as planned. But we don't live in a perfect world! Now, I try to prioritize in a better fashion to avoid pitfalls.

What Grandma said:

Do it today; why wait?

Tomorrow you might not remember to do it.

Time to do it is now; let's go.

Don't just sit there or there. You got to do something.

If you don't do, you don't get the something you want.

Don't do? Who knows what bad will happen.

It won't get done without you.

What Grandma said:

So, when are you going to cut the
grass, when it's a foot high?

Study—don't cram the night before a test.

Time goes by so fast. So what are you waiting for?

You're wasting so much time—start already!

If you don't fix your bike pedal before you
go riding, you could fall off your bike.

If other people get there before you, you might miss out.

Memory:

One day when my mother and father went out for the day, they gave me the task of pulling weeds out of the flower beds in the back yard. I really wasn't very enthused about the task, so I told myself that I had to do other important things first. I ate lunch, did homework, talked on the telephone with friends, ate ice cream, and read a comic book. I wanted to do anything but pick weeds. Morning turned into afternoon, which then began to turn into dusk.

My mother and father were due home in the early evening. During my reverie, my grandmother asked, "Wer here seam mir?" ("Who is going to do it? Not me.") I realized that my grandmother was talking to me and that if I continued to be inactive, the garden would not be weeded. And so, realizing that it was my responsibility, I began to understand that if I did not do it, it would not get done—and it needed to be done!

I try to utilize my grandmother's wisdom most of the time, because I know that her advice is sound, but sometimes I get lazy. Grandma would tell me that it is okay but that I should become "unlazy"! If she were here today I would tell her that I was far from perfect. I know that she loved me unconditionally, so there would not be a problem admitting the truth to her.

Encouragement and Support

We all need love, encouragement, and support to thrive, grow, and get our needs met. We need somebody there to support us when times are difficult. As a child, my mother was emotionally unavailable. Even though my father called me his "little butterball," he was always working and did not spend a great deal of time nurturing his family. But I did have a charismatic and supportive individual in my life, a positive force who made all the difference—my Bubbie!

One day, I decided to make chocolate chip cookies for my class. I started the project, but after the third ingredient it did not seem as much fun as I had thought. I spread flour all over the kitchen. It went up my nose, and I began to cough. When I went to clean up the mess I had made, I knocked over the bag of sugar. I was grunting. My grandmother heard me, and she also started to sneeze.

Even though she did not see the actual mess, she realized that I was not very happy. I left all of the stuff in the kitchen and went into my bedroom because I was so frustrated. I guess my grandmother knew that I would not be going into the kitchen soon. She sat by my bed and said, *"Nischt alts takhles vi veln nikhtik; nischt farlozn, -- -- ich gleybn du."* ("Not everything goes as planned, and it's okay, but I really believe in you.")

She had a glass of tea, and I had a cookie and milk. She put on the radio, and the music was soothing. I then cleaned up the mess, continued with the recipe, and made delicious cookies that I brought to school. I felt good about myself, especially when my grandmother said to me, *"Ich visn du matshiek zany shtoltsim."* ("See, I knew you could do it. I'm so proud of you.")

It seemed as though my grandmother had a sixth sense for what was going on around her. I did not even have to ask her for support. She seemed to instinctively know when encouragement was necessary. Even though she thought I was wonderful, she always provided constructive criticism and made me accountable for the good, bad, and the ugly. The wonderful thing was that she loved me unconditionally.

No matter how disappointed she may have been regarding something that I had done, I never dreaded her arrival or constructive criticism. I knew that she wanted me to love myself, to have good values, to be responsible, to be charitable, and to have a voice that would be heard. No matter what the situation was, good or bad, she always ended by giving me a hug, touching my face and saying, *"Shelenkeh, Shelenkeh."* ("Sheila, my Sheila.")

What Grandma said:

You can do it if you really try, you'll make it.

Grandma is always here to make it better.

You're never too old to try something new.

I'll kiss it and make better. I'm so proud.

Of course you can do it, don't think different.

It's never too late, you know.

So, start over!

Always try to look on the bright side
of things; see it half full.

Listen, half a loaf is better than no loaf.

Don't let them make you cry; you're
just as good as they are.

What Grandma said:

Don't even listen to him; he's a big bully.

You can do whatever you put your mind to.

It's okay to dream ... dreams may come true.

Of course you will be able to do that.

You're the best.

Grandma is always here for you; tell Grandma anything.

I might not like your behavior, but I will always love you, no matter what.

It'll all work out in the end; wait, you'll see.

It's really not as bad as it seems.

Everybody has their share of problems; you're not alone.

Everything will look so much better in the morning.

Memory:

I had to make my own dress for a fashion show that my sewing class was presenting. My friends and I were very excited! We were making our own patterns, taking measurements of each other, and coordinating fabrics. My dress was to be made of a gold and white cotton fabric. Accents were to be in a red fabric, also cotton. It took months of diligent planning and working. The day finally arrived when we had to try on our handmade dresses. If I could think of a word stronger than hideous I would use it. A genuine potato sack would have looked better! I cried for days. (I guess I was negative a great deal of the time because, in retrospect, I always seem to have been crying!)

One week before the show, my grandmother told me to put on the dress. I explained that there was nothing that could be done and that I would just be humiliated. I couldn't resist her sweet voice coaxing me to just try the dress on once more. She moved her hands on the shoulders of the dress, then around the waist, onto the pockets, and finally to the hem. She used her thumb to start measuring how much to take in the fabric. She used safety pins to pinpoint locations that needed some alteration. I knew that she would not be able to make the alterations herself. Knitting and crocheting, yes, but sewing, no.

So what was she doing? She told me that I was going to fix the dress by myself and that she would be my guide. Of course, I was not amenable or cooperative. She finally said to me, "Men hobn zeit, arbet, baldik." ("You have time—work. It's early; I know you can do it. It's possible.") She didn't see my lopsided dress as a "fait accompli." Rather, she saw it as an opportunity to take action. What she was trying to tell me was that I could be a part of the problem or part of the solution. She was absolutely correct! I reworked the dress, with her advice, and I was a big hit in the fashion show! Now I always look for remedies instead of simply lamenting!

Being Grateful and Giving Thanks

While it is important to have goals and strive for additional achievements, it is important to be grateful for what we do have and to not complain about what we do not have. It is also important to help less fortunate individuals. Jerry Lewis was once asked why he repeatedly worked with the Muscular Dystrophy Foundation, and his reply was, "What you keep you lose; what you lose you keep forever."

As a child, I never really understood those words, but I did realize that they were powerful, so I wrote them on a small piece of paper and taped it to my night table. It was only after my dearest, beloved grandmother passed away and was lost to me that I realized the meaning of those vital words. Even though her physical presence was no longer with me and I was unable to feel her smooth fingers caress the outlines of my face, I knew that the legacy of life that she had left me would remain with me, in my heart, for all of my own lifetime. Though I still feel her loss, I also feel her gain and am grateful for the precious time that we spent together.

I remember that every day while eating breakfast my grandmother would say the same thing to us: *"Zayn dankbar fil."* ("Be grateful for what you have; it's so much.") Even today, when I eat breakfast I smile and remember her words. That always begins my day on a positive note. As I write this book I am so grateful to have had a woman of valor, such as my grandmother, in my life. Thank you, thank you, my dearest, darling beloved Bubbie.

What Grandma said:

You ought to be grateful to him for what he did for you.

Be happy with what you have.

Stop looking at what other people have;
be grateful for what you have.

You're lucky he's your friend; he's so caring.

If you don't get it the first time, do it again.

Be happy for what you have, and don't
worry about what you don't have.

Some people have more, some less.

Always give thanks for the things you
have and the people in your life.

Don't just think of yourself; don't be selfish.

You want him to share with you, so
you better share with him.

Don't forget to say *thank you*; it's so important.

Memory:

My grandmother used to knit and crochet all the time, even though she was blind. She made scarves, doilies, and tablecloths. I still don't know how she did it! One day she said to me, "Sezn sich, eins tog men dankin me." ("Sit down. One day you will thank me for this, you'll see.") I had no idea what she wanted from me. She handed me two knitting needles and a ball of yarn. She began to give me instructions; it was very difficult for me. My hand-eye coordination was not working too well. At one point she repeated her instructions, and I became so frustrated that I took the stitches off the needle instead of doing what she explained. She immediately asked me why I had done that. Maybe she really wasn't blind after all. (Actually, she stopped hearing the clicking of the needles.)

After awhile, she encouraged me to have a glass of milk and a cookie to calm down. When I finished my snack she went right back to her tutelage. She then said, "Mein seam farlosn, zogn dankn." ("You're not a quitter—be grateful.")

I had no idea what she was trying to tell me. But I soon realized that if I stopped complaining and started listening, I might actually have a talent. Once I knew what I was doing, I began to make scarves and hats for all my friends, who thought I was a genius. My grandmother was trying to tell me that I must listen to others who are wiser than I, persevere in the face of adversity, and, above all, be grateful to others for their help. Even today, as I cast the initial yarn on the knitting needle to make scarves and hats for my own family, I am grateful to my grandmother and thank her for teaching me this wonderful skill!

Mind Your Own Business

Too often we become enmeshed and embroiled in other people's lives. We tend to give advice and sometimes even seek to control the situation. While it is appropriate to be nurturing and supportive and to give advice if asked, it is also important to let others live their own lives without our interference. My grandmother was always telling us *"Farsorgn nos klor."* ("Keep your nose clear.") She did not engage in gossip or spread nasty rumors. I knew that if I told her something in confidence, she would respect my privacy (as long as there was no element of danger).

Her beliefs stemmed from her ocean voyage to the United States. She often told me that people fought constantly and spread stories and meddled in other people's affairs. I remembered her teaching. One day at work while I ate lunch in the hospital cafeteria, two of my colleagues had a disagreement. It began innocuously but then escalated into screaming and yelling.

All of the doctors and nurses began to focus on our table. When the combatants asked me to settle their issue and tell them who was right and who was wrong, I remembered my grandmother's words. I stood up, wished the ladies good luck, and said, "You are on your own."

By the time I reached my office, the gossip was in full swing. When the staff tried to ask me questions about the altercation, I merely said, "No comment." The gossip continued, and individuals began taking sides. A great deal of anger and hurt followed. I was glad that I had listened to my grandmother. I knew that it was one of her better lessons when I overheard a colleague say, "Boy, that Sheila never gets in trouble; she never gossips, and she can keep a secret!"

What Grandma said:

They're not talking about you, so stay out of it.

Listen, don't spread nasty rumors.

Don't listen to that gossip.

Keep the secret; don't blab it all over the place.

This is not your business; it's theirs so stay out of it.

Don't eaves drop; it's their private business and none of yours.

Hang up the telephone. It's not for you.

Memory:

One day when I was a child our telephone rang, and my mother and I picked up different phones at the same time. Apparently, she and my dad were having some kind of disagreement. They did not know that I was still on the line, and I decided to eavesdrop. My grandmother came into the kitchen, where I was holding the phone to my ear. Since she could not see and I was not talking, I thought that I could get away with my little scheme.

I swear that woman had radar! Very calmly, she said, "Asoi, wer areimmarn? Keener nit, opschatal." ("So who are you fooling? Nobody, so stop already.") I was astounded and taken aback. The tone of her voice let me know that eavesdropping, meddling in other's business, and carrying gossip were definitely verboten! Even today, if I'm tempted to gossip, I become that little girl in the kitchen, and I keep my mouth shut!

So how did she know that I was doing something underhanded? She knew that I was in the kitchen and realized that she did not hear my footsteps or movements, so it seemed likely to her that I must have been doing something sneaky. I could never get away with doing anything unscrupulous when my grandmother was around. So eventually I stopped trying!

How to Handle Money

We cannot live in this world without money. We must work hard in school so that we can get a good job. (Hopefully, there won't be a recession.) While making money is important, my grandmother taught me that it should not be my only focus in life. She always said, *"Nor gelt."* ("Not just for money.") We won't often hear a man on his death bed say, "I wish that I had stayed home less and worked harder to make more money." It is important to save and spend money wisely; always keep a reserve in case of bad times.

As a teenager, my son wanted to be a foreign exchange student. He filled out the copious amount of required paperwork and was accepted. He was elated! Then a terrorist attack came, bringing an element of danger. We told my son that he was not allowed to go. He asked if he could go to boarding school in Colorado instead. We agreed, but since it cost more money, we told my son that he had to get a job to earn the difference.

He secured a job with a gardener who worked in the area where we lived. My friends were shocked when they saw my son lifting bales of cut grass into the enormous truck. I thought, *Hard work never killed anyone—not me or his dad*. It was a good lesson, because my son decided that manual labor was not for him. He decided to work with his brain instead of his brawn. He is quite a success today, working with his brain!

Friends wanted know why we insisted on having him work when we could afford the difference in cost. My husband and I were unconcerned about the gossip. Every time a friend asked, "Why?" we responded, "Why not?" My grandmother always said, *"Shver arbetn gut neshome."* ("Hard work doesn't hurt; it's good for the soul.")

Her words were so poignant that we sought to heed her advice and wisdom. Even today, amidst a world that is so frenetic, my children take nothing for granted. They understand the value of hard work, and I am so proud of them!

What Grandma said:

You can't go outside and take the
money from the trees.

If you save all the pennies, soon you will have a dollar.

Money alone doesn't make happiness,
and it can't buy health.

Better save for a rainy day; don't let
the money go to your head.

Don't be foolish and waste money; it's too hard to get.

Work hard and the rest will come;
don't just chase dollars.

Save a little, spend a little, but give to charity.

That's not free! I have to pay for it first.

I'm putting money in your piggy bank.

What Grandma said:

Don't waste your time on that. You could be doing something else and making money for yourself.

Come, let's go to the bank and open up an account for you.

Be careful with your money; keep it in your pocket.

Don't buy that—too expensive; cheaper at Woolworth's.

Don't worry so much about the dollars and cents; better to worry more about the sense.

Don't worry about the money; if you're healthy, you are wealthy.

Do the best job, even if sweeping the floor; good will come of it.

Memory:

My grandmother believed that money in and of itself was important, but her focus was more on how to use the money wisely: work hard for it, save some, and give some to charity. One day the chain on my bicycle broke. When I asked my father to take me to the bicycle shop, he told me that I would have to pay for the chain myself. I was too young to work, so I just moped around the house lamenting about not being able to ride my bike. My grandmother came over to me and said, "Fregn arbet, beser gelt." ("Ask for work, better to get money.") She was trying to tell me that complaining would not help me and that my time would be better spent trying to earn the money to get it fixed.

So I asked my mother if I could do some chores for her: set the table, vacuum, help with laundry, clean the bathroom. My mother thought it was a great idea, and I made enough money to fix my bicycle. This taught me that complaining was a waste of time and that time would be better spent in a more productive manner. Even today, when I am folding laundry I sometimes remember that I got paid for doing those chores. My grandmother taught me to think about solutions rather than prolong the problem.

Life's Lesson's

We come into this world as a *tabular rasa*. We learn how to become human through socialization by significant others. We need a license to drive a car or get married, but there is no course available to an individual that will provide a license for effective life skills. Grandma is the closest we come to that!

My grandmother was the most important person in my life. This book would never had been written had she not been my rock, my foundation. She was loving and kind but provided constructive criticism. She helped me to understand that free will was part of life, but it also required responsibility. She taught me to appreciate how each individual is special in his own right and is part of a larger entity of which he or she is an integral component.

She taught me that life was precious but that it was hard work.

And that living was never static; rather it evolved, moving on a continuum from birth to death. I understood that I grew not only physically, but psychologically as well. She made me realize that if I did not love myself, I would not be able to deal with the trials and tribulations of life, of which there are many. I now understand how the wisdom of my grandmother's teachings has made me who I am today. While my life is filled with many good things, there are many challenges that I deal with on a daily basis. While I cannot change what has already happened, I can work toward making new things happen.

I try to live like the lady that my Grandma taught me to be. I don't use judgmental words, such as *good, bad, always, never, should, shouldn't, right,* and *wrong*. I have established boundaries that are comfortable for me, and I have no trouble saying "No" instead of "Yes." I have longstanding relationships that I treasure. I always give freely and lovingly to others. I consider others' needs as well as my own and am willing to collaborate on issues that may be in dispute. While my intention is not to deliberately hurt others, I am human and I have foibles, and that is okay. But I am always willing to take responsibility for something that I have done to another and am always willing to apologize. I believe that all of life is sacred. As such, we deserve a world full of peace. That cannot happen without each one of us playing an important role to make our world loving and stable.

My grandmother contributed to this world not only with her words, but through her deeds as well. I hope that my grandchildren will be able to say the same about me. I try to teach them not to take anything for granted. In addition, I tell them to persevere in the face of tremendous adversity and to be kind to themselves first, so that they may be kind to others. I have given my children roots and wings, and they know that my home is always a place they can return to and find love.

Out of everything bad comes something good: my children are both strong and independent. My son chose to go to boarding school in Lugano, Switzerland, so that he could experience another culture first hand. My daughter received her doctorate and then traveled around the world for one year by herself. A mother's nightmare! When I told my daughter that I would worry greatly while she was traveling, she told me that I was the one who made her believe that she would never be alone because she always had me, myself, and I with her and that she could climb every mountain. I guess she really took me literally because she climbed Kathmandu in Nepal.

My own words to my children and grandchildren are, "If it is to be, it is up to me." I not only love my children and grandchildren, I like who they are. The mates that my children have chosen are wonderful human beings, and I am delighted to have them in the family. Many parents are disappointed in their children, but I have raised children of whom I am very proud. I hope that one day they might feel a bit about me the way I feel about my grandmother.

Though I have the benefit of sight, I hope that I will continue to see the world around me as clearly as my blind grandmother saw it. I try to pass on what she considered to be very important: family, honor, trust, dignity, love, peace on earth, peace of mind, and respect for self and others.

Time to say au revoir for now, Bubbie—but not good-bye.

What Grandma said:

Be good to yourself.

Don't make judgments before you
know all what's going on.

You need to love yourself first. They you
can start to love other people.

Time goes by so fast. When the time is good, do it.

Take a vacation, you need to rest
and have a good time.

We can plan but we don't really
know what will happen to us.

Always try to keep trying.

From failures, we make successes.

Try to learn from what didn't work.

Be happy with yourself; you did a good job.

What Grandma said:

Don't cry when you spill the milk.

Make some nice friends that you can count on.

Keep writing it down; then you can go back and see what you wrote.

Life always goes up and down.

Remember after you fall down, you get up.

Oy, if I only knew then what I know now.

Think about everything you might be able to do.

Don't be nasty to everyone trying to help you.

It is important to give to the poor; they need help.

It can't always be your way.

This is no court so stop being a judge.

What Grandma said:

You can't always be first.

You can't have everything you want; nobody can.

Don't believe everything you hear.

Don't do it for me; do it for yourself.

If you don't do it first and you want
to do it, try some more.

You've got to like yourself first.

In this world, people need love.

Make someone happy.

If you give others then you feel good about it.

You need to make the foundation first. Then,
go build the house; it won't fall down.

Memory:

My friends and I were building things out of blocks on the wooden floor in my bedroom. We were trying to build a house by placing one single block on top of another single block. They kept falling down and making a racket. My friends loved my grandmother, so she had no qualms about coming into my room and sitting on the floor with us. She asked what we were trying to accomplish. She told us to show her what we were doing. My friends asked her how we might do that because she could not see. She replied, "Ober, kenen hern, tapn." ("But I can hear and feel.")

She told us to continue what we were doing. After the third block was placed on the top of the other two single blocks, she put her hands on the blocks and said to us, "On untn nit oibn." ("Without a bottom, there can be no top.") She made a foundation of three blocks, side by side, for several rows. She then repeated it with two blocks and then with one block. Our house was beautiful and stood tall. What she was trying to tell us was that one needs a sturdy foundation for everything, including making life work for us.

There is a great deal of new construction in Florida. Every time that I see a foundation being poured in concrete I think of my grandmother, who will always be the foundation, the rock, of my soul—as well as the angel on my shoulder!

CPSIA information can be obtained at www.ICGtesting.com
Printed in the USA
LVOW062022021012
301203LV00002B/246/P